WEST AFRICA

WEST AFRICA

1880 TO THE PRESENT: A CULTURAL PATCHWORK

DANIEL E. HARMON

INTRODUCTORY ESSAY BY
Dr. Richard E. Leakey
Chairman, Wildlife Clubs
of Kenya Association
✢
AFTERWORD BY
Deirdre Shields

CHELSEA HOUSE PUBLISHERS
Philadelphia
In association with Covos Day Books, South Africa

CHELSEA HOUSE PUBLISHERS

EDITOR IN CHIEF Sally Cheney
PRODUCTION MANAGER Kim Shinners
ART DIRECTOR Sara Davis
ASSOCIATE ART DIRECTOR Takeshi Takahashi
SERIES DESIGNER Keith Trego
COVER DESIGN Emiliano Begnardi

The Chelsea House World Wide Web address is http://www.chelseahouse.com

First Printing

1 3 5 7 9 8 6 4 2

Library of Congress Cataloging-in-Publication Data Applied for.

ISBN 0-7910-5748-8

The photographs in this book are from the Royal Geographical Society Picture Library. Most are being published for the first time.

The Royal Geographical Society Picture Library provides an unrivaled source of over half a million images of peoples and landscapes from around the globe. Photographs date from the 1840s onwards on a variety of subjects including the British Colonial Empire, deserts, exploration, indigenous peoples, landscapes, remote destinations, and travel.

Photography, beginning with the daguerreotype in 1839, is only marginally younger than the Society, which encouraged its explorers to use the new medium from its earliest days. From the remarkable mid-19th century black-and-white photographs to color transparencies of the late 20th century, the focus of the collection is not the generic stock shot but the portrayal of man's resilience, adaptability, and mobility in remote parts of the world.

In organizing this project, we have incurred many debts of gratitude. Our first, though, is to the professional staff of the Picture Library for their generous assistance, especially to Joanna Scadden, Picture Library Manager.

CONTENTS

Exploration of Africa: The Emerging Nations

THE DARK CONTINENT

DR. RICHARD E. LEAKEY

THE CONCEPT OF AFRICAN exploration has been greatly influenced by the hero status given to the European adventurers and missionaries who went off to Africa in the last century. Their travels and travails were certainly extraordinary and nobody can help but be impressed by the tremendous physical and intellectual courage that was so much a characteristic of people such as Livingstone, Stanley, Speke, and Baker, to name just a few. The challenges and rewards that Africa offered, both in terms of commerce and also "saved souls," inspired people to take incredible risks and endure personal suffering to a degree that was probably unique to the exploration of Africa.

I myself was fortunate enough to have had the opportunity to organize one or two minor expeditions to remote spots in Africa where there were no roads or airfields and marching with porters and/or camels was the best option at the time. I have also had the thrill of being with people untouched and often unmoved by contact with Western or other technologically based cultures, and these experiences remain for me amongst the most exciting and salutary of my life. With the contemporary revolution in technology, there will be few if any such opportunities again. Indeed I often find myself slightly saddened by the realization that were life ever discovered on another planet, exploration would doubtless be done by remote sensing and making full use of artificial, digital intelligence. At least it is unlikely to be in my lifetime and this is a relief!

WEST AFRICA

Notwithstanding all of this, I believe that the age of exploration and discovery in Africa is far from over. The future offers incredible opportunities for new discoveries that will push back the frontiers of knowledge. This endeavor will of course not involve exotic and arduous journeys into malaria-infested tropical swamps, but it will certainly require dedication, team work, public support, and a conviction that the rewards to be gained will more than justify the efforts and investment.

EARLY EXPLORERS

Many of us were raised and educated at school with the belief that Africa, the so-called Dark Continent, was actually discovered by early European travelers and explorers. The date of this "discovery" is difficult to establish, and anyway a distinction has always had to be drawn between northern Africa and the vast area south of the Sahara. The Romans certainly had information about the continent's interior as did others such as the Greeks. A diverse range of traders ventured down both the west coast and the east coast from at least the ninth century, and by the tenth century Islam had taken root in a number of new towns and settlements established by Persian and Arab interests along the eastern tropical shores. Trans-African trade was probably under way well before this time, perhaps partly stimulated by external interests.

Close to the beginning of the first millennium, early Christians were establishing the Coptic church in the ancient kingdom of Ethiopia and at other coastal settlements along Africa's northern Mediterranean coast. Along the west coast of Africa, European trade in gold, ivory, and people was well established by the sixteenth century. Several hundred years later, early in the 19th century, the systematic penetration and geographical exploration of Africa was undertaken by Europeans seeking geographical knowledge and territory and looking for opportunities not only for commerce but for the chance to spread the Gospel. The extraordinary narratives of some of the journeys of early European travelers and adventurers in Africa are a vivid reminder of just how recently Africa has become embroiled in the power struggles and vested interests of non-Africans.

THE DARK CONTINENT

AFRICA'S GIFT TO THE WORLD

My own preoccupation over the past thirty years has been to study human prehistory, and from this perspective it is very clear that Africa was never "discovered" in the sense in which so many people have been and, perhaps, still are being taught. Rather, it was Africans themselves who found that there was a world beyond their shores.

Prior to about two million years ago, the only humans or proto-humans in existence were confined to Africa; as yet, the remaining world had not been exposed to this strange mammalian species, which in time came to dominate the entire planet. It is no trivial matter to recognize the cultural implications that arise from this entirely different perspective of Africa and its relationship to the rest of humanity.

How many of the world's population grow up knowing that it was in fact African people who first moved and settled in southern Europe and Central Asia and migrated to the Far East? How many know that Africa's principal contribution to the world is in fact humanity itself? These concepts are quite different from the notion that Africa was only "discovered" in the past few hundred years and will surely change the commonly held idea that somehow Africa is a "laggard," late to come onto the world stage.

It could be argued that our early human forebears—the *Homo erectus* who moved out of Africa—have little or no bearing on the contemporary world and its problems. I disagree and believe that the often pejorative thoughts that are associated with the Dark Continent and dark skins, as well as with the general sense that Africans are somehow outside the mainstream of human achievement, would be entirely negated by the full acceptance of a universal African heritage for all of humanity. This, after all, is the truth that has now been firmly established by scientific inquiry.

The study of human origins and prehistory will surely continue to be important in a number of regions of Africa and this research must continue to rank high on the list of relevant ongoing exploration and discovery. There is still much to be learned about the early stages of human development, and the age of the "first humans"—the first bipedal apes—has not been firmly established. The current hypothesis is that prior to five million years ago there were no bipeds, and this would mean that humankind is only five million years old. Beyond Africa, there were no humans until just two million years ago, and this is a consideration that political leaders and people as a whole need to bear in mind.

RECENT HISTORY

When it comes to the relatively recent history of Africa's contemporary people, there is still considerable ignorance. The evidence suggests that there were major migrations of people within the continent during the past 5,000 years, and the impact of the introduction of domestic stock must have been quite considerable on the way of life of many of Africa's people. Early settlements and the beginnings of nation states are, as yet, poorly researched and recorded. Although archaeological studies have been undertaken in Africa for well over a hundred years, there remain more questions than answers.

One question of universal interest concerns the origin and inspiration for the civilization of early Egypt. The Nile has, of course, offered opportunities for contacts between the heart of Africa and the Mediterranean seacoast, but very little is known about human settlement and civilization in the upper reaches of the Blue and White Nile between 4,000 and 10,000 years ago. We do know that the present Sahara Desert is only about 10,000 years old; before this Central Africa was wetter and more fertile, and research findings have shown that it was only during the past 10,000 years that Lake Turkana in the northern Kenya was isolated from the Nile system. When connected, it would have been an excellent connection between the heartland of the continent and the Mediterranean.

Another question focuses on the extensive stone-walled villages and towns in Southern Africa. The Great Zimbabwe is but one of thousands of standing monuments in East, Central, and Southern Africa that attest to considerable human endeavor in Africa long before contact with Europe or Arabia. The Neolithic period and Iron Age still offer very great opportunities for exploration and discovery.

As an example of the importance of history, let us look at the modern South Africa where a visitor might still be struck by the not-too-subtle representation of a past that, until a few years ago, only "began" with the arrival of Dutch settlers some 400 years back. There are, of course, many pre-Dutch sites, including extensive fortified towns where kingdoms and nation states had thrived hundreds of years before contact with Europe; but this evidence has been poorly documented and even more poorly portrayed.

Few need to be reminded of the sparseness of Africa's precolonial written history. There are countless cultures and historical narratives that have been recorded only as oral history and legend. As postcolonial Africa further consolidates itself, history must be reviewed and deepened to incorporate the realities of precolonial human settlement as well as foreign contact. Africa's identity and self-respect is closely linked to this.

One of the great tragedies is that African history was of little interest to the early European travelers who were in a hurry and had no brief to document the details of the people they came across during their travels. In the basements of countless European museums, there are stacked shelves of African "curios"—objects taken from the people but seldom documented in terms of the objects' use, customs, and history.

There is surely an opportunity here for contemporary scholars to do something. While much of Africa's precolonial past has been obscured by the slave trade, colonialism, evangelism, and modernization, there remains an opportunity, at least in some parts of the continent, to record what still exists. This has to be one of the most vital frontiers for African exploration and discovery as we approach the end of this millennium. Some of the work will require trips to the field, but great gains could be achieved by a systematic and coordinated effort to record the inventories of European museums and archives. The Royal Geographical Society could well play a leading role in this chapter of African exploration. The compilation of a central data bank on what is known and what exists would, if based on a coordinated initiative to record the customs and social organization of Africa's remaining indigenous peoples, be a huge contribution to the heritage of humankind.

MEDICINES AND FOODS

On the African continent itself, there remain countless other areas for exploration and discovery. Such endeavors will be achieved without the fanfare of great expeditions and high adventure as was the case during the last century and they should, as far as possible, involve exploration and discovery of African frontiers by Africans themselves. These frontiers are not geographic: they are boundaries of knowledge in the sphere of Africa's home-grown cultures and natural world.

Indigenous knowledge is a very poorly documented subject in many parts of the world, and Africa is a prime example of a continent where centuries of accumulated local knowledge is rapidly disappearing in the face of modernization. I believe, for example, that there is much to be learned about the use of wild African plants for both medicinal and nutritional purposes. Such knowledge, kept to a large extent as the experience and memory of elders in various indigenous communities, could potentially have far-reaching benefits for Africa and for humanity as a whole.

The importance of new remedies based on age-old medicines cannot be underestimated. Over the past two decades, international companies have begun to take note and to exploit certain African plants for pharmacological preparations. All too often, Africa has not been the beneficiary of these "discoveries," which are, in most instances, nothing more than the refinement and improvement of traditional African medicine. The opportunities for exploration and discovery in this area are immense and will have assured economic return on investment. One can only hope that such work will be in partnership with the people of Africa and not at the expense of the continent's best interests.

Within the same context, there is much to be learned about the traditional knowledge of the thousands of plants that have been utilized by different African communities for food. The contemporary world has become almost entirely dependent, in terms of staple foods, on the cultivation of only six principal plants: corn, wheat, rice, yams, potatoes, and bananas. This cannot be a secure basis to guarantee the food requirements of more than five billion people.

Many traditional food plants in Africa are drought resistant and might well offer new alternatives for large-scale agricultural development in the years to come. Crucial to this development is finding out what African people used before exotics were introduced. In some rural areas of the continent, it is still possible to learn about much of this by talking to the older generation. It is certainly a great shame that some of the early European travelers in Africa were ill equipped to study and record details of diet and traditional plant use, but I am sure that, although it is late, it is not too late. The compilation of a pan-African database on what is known about the use of the continent's plant resources is a vital matter requiring action.

VANISHING SPECIES

In the same spirit, there is as yet a very incomplete inventory of the continent's other species. The inevitable trend of bringing land into productive management is resulting in the loss of unknown but undoubtedly large numbers of species. This genetic resource may be invaluable to the future of Africa and indeed humankind, and there really is a need for coordinated efforts to record and understand the continent's biodiversity.

In recent years important advances have been made in the study of tropical ecosystems in Central and South America, and I am sure that similar endeavors in Africa would be rewarding. At present, Africa's semi-arid and highland ecosystems are better understood than the more diverse and complex lowland forests, which are themselves under particular threat from loggers and farmers. The challenges of exploring the biodiversity of the upper canopy in the tropical forests, using the same techniques that are now used in Central American forests, are fantastic and might also lead to eco-tourist developments for these areas in the future.

It is indeed an irony that huge amounts of money are being spent by the advanced nations in an effort to discover life beyond our own planet, while at the same time nobody on this planet knows the extent and variety of life here at home. The tropics are especially relevant in this regard and one can only hope that Africa will become the focus of renewed efforts of research on biodiversity and tropical ecology.

AN AFROCENTRIC VIEW

Overall, the history of Africa has been presented from an entirely Eurocentric or even Caucasocentric perspective, and until recently this has not been adequately reviewed. The penetration of Africa, especially during the last century, was important in its own way; but today the realities of African history, art, culture, and politics are better known. The time has come to regard African history in terms of what has happened in Africa itself, rather than simply in terms of what non-African individuals did when they first traveled to the continent.

Banjul, Gambia c. 1890. *The nation of Gambia is a strip of land 15–30 miles wide and about 180 miles long on either side of the Gambia River. Except for its coastline, it is surrounded by Senegal. Its unusual shape and size resulted from nineteenth-century territorial agreements between Great Britain and France arising from their rivalry in West Africa. Peanuts, which have been exported from Gambia since 1830, account for 95 percent of the country's commerce. This photograph is of Trader's Wharf, Banjul (formerly Bathurst), capital and the Atlantic port of Gambia. The city is on St. Mary's Island near the mouth of the Gambia River. It was founded in 1816 as a British military post on the river to suppress the slave trade. More than half the current population (2000 est. 60,000) is Wolof, a Muslim people from Senegal. The Aku, descendants of freed slaves, are a significant minority.*

INTRODUCTION

To West African natives, Mungo Park was a laughable curiosity. They huddled round him, touching his hair and his pale European face, pulling at the yellow buttons on his clothes. Who was this strangely dressed, strange-looking, strange-speaking visitor? What should they do with him? He wished to travel deep into the interior of their continent, into territories little known even to them. Perhaps he was a god; perhaps he was just a deranged mortal, come from a faraway land on some preposterous errand. Should they provide him with guides, or wash their hands of him (after relieving him of his possessions—particularly those bewitching buttons)?

The year was 1795, and Park was no rugged, veteran explorer but a young Scottish surgeon. He had been to the East Indies once as a ship's doctor and had made useful studies of the wildlife he had encountered there. Adventurous by nature, he then had answered the call of the newly formed African Association in London. The association had heard just enough of the River Niger to know it should be fully explored, for the Niger apparently was one of Africa's major watercourses. Where did it originate? Where, exactly, did it empty into the sea? Was it linked to the Nile, far to the east?

Park had arrived only a few months earlier in what is now Gambia, on the western coast of Africa's "bulge," and done what he could to educate himself quickly. He had learned a little of the language and customs of the Mandingo people, then set forth with a couple of servant/interpreters up the River Gambia. He'd brought bags of beads, tobacco, and other trading items. At the river village of Pisania he had struck off into the heartland, hoping to come to the larger river. Now that he was among the natives, he was unsure of his reception— and not a little embarrassed.

A local chief warned him not to continue. Previous white travelers, the chief said, had been lost, contracted tropical fevers, even been murdered. Undeterred, Park found guides and plunged northward into the land of the Moors, Arab peoples who dominated the sub-Saharan steppes and beyond. Soon Moorish robbers fell upon his party when they stopped for water. Park's native companions deserted him, and he spent terrifying nights listening to the cries of wild beasts roaming the darkness. Then, out of nowhere, another band of Moors suddenly attacked and dragged him away to their leader.

The Moors took virtually everything he had, kept him in a pigpen, fed him barely enough to survive, and threatened him with torture and death. Desperate, he escaped . . . and found himself totally at the mercy of the Dark Continent. Groping his way by instinct toward friendlier environs, he was battered by a sandstorm, lashed by a tempest, and attacked by still another band of Moors who stole his cloak.

Park was a pitiful figure entering the region of the River Niger. Here, the people were poor but welcomed him to share their simple meals. He regained a bit of strength and pushed a little way farther along the river. He realized, though, that his explorations had proceeded as far as they could for the present. He had expended all his energy, his trade goods, his resources, and his health simply *reaching* the Niger. Charting its course would have to come later.

Where did this eastward-flowing river—"the great water," as the natives called it—lead? he asked tribal merchants. No one knew. Probably, they told him, it flowed to the end of the world. . . .

Introduction

The African Association received Park back in England as a hero. He wrote a book describing the bizarre customs, beautiful forests, and unforeseen hardships of West Africa. It was the outside world's first detailed picture of that alluring region. Several years later, the young doctor would return to navigate the Niger—and would succumb to the river's hazards, disappearing under mysterious and disturbing circumstances in 1806.

In the coming century, the people of the West African interior would see much more of Park's successors than they wanted.

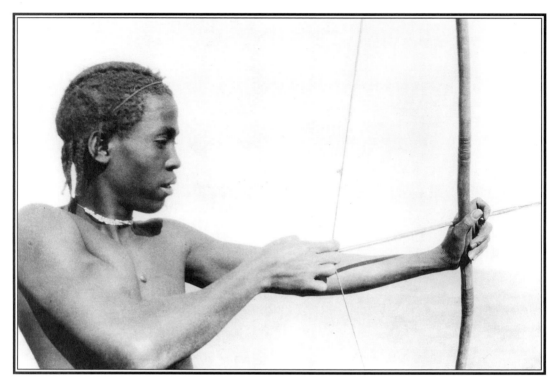

Hunter, Chad 1932. *Chad is one of the world's poorest countries. It is a landlocked state in central Africa. Most of the people in this remote, desolate area live by rudimentary farming or as nomads. Today Chad has an average of about one radio for every four people and about one television set for every 850. More than 100 different languages and dialects are spoken. Political, social, and religious differences between the Muslim peoples of the north and the peoples of the south—most of whom follow traditional African religions or Christianity—have kept Chad in nearly a constant state of civil war since the mid-1960s. Indeed, the tapestry of languages, peoples, and religions in Chad underscores that it is a crossroads of cultural interchange. The population density (est. 2000) is about 10 persons per square mile. Almost 50 percent of the population is younger than age 15, and life expectancy here is one of the world's lowest.*

A Land of
Enchantment . . .
and Hazards

Look at Africa on a globe. Instantly, you will notice its vast "bulge" into the Atlantic Ocean. This is the region geographers call West Africa. More accurately, the bulge might be called "Northwest Africa." West Africa commonly refers, however, not to the continent's central and southern Atlantic coastline, but only to the massive northwestward arc from the Gulf of Guinea up and around, halfway to the Strait of Gibraltar that separates Africa from Spain.

Some reference books continue the boundary of West Africa all the way to the strait itself, and beyond, absorbing hundreds of miles of the lower Mediterranean shoreline. Roughly, this larger definition draws a south-north line through northern Africa that lops off the "bulge." It begins at the lower coast between Cameroon and Nigeria and follows the border between those two countries northward. It then extends along the Chad/Niger border, then the Libya/Algeria border, then the Libya/Tunisia border. All the land to the west, broadly speaking, is West Africa—20 countries, some 3 million square miles.

Historians and political observers, though, usually exclude from their definition of West Africa the Sahara Desert nations—Western Sahara, Morocco, Algeria, and Tunisia—which they consider to be part of North Africa. Likewise, Niger, Mali, and

Mauritania often are regarded as part of North Africa. At the same time, the lands enveloping the River Niger—most prominently, Niger and Nigeria—in many ways constitute a region unto themselves, separate from western, northern, and central Africa.

On the other hand, some scholars reach farther eastward and southward in their definitions of West Africa, including, for example, Cameroon and Chad.

In short, if you consult several encyclopedias or other sources, you well may find several different sets of boundaries for "West Africa." For our study, we will define West Africa as 17 nations: Benin, Burkina Faso, the Cape Verde Islands, Côte d'Ivoire, The Gambia, Ghana, Guinea, Guinea-Bissau, Liberia, Mali, Mauritania, Niger, Nigeria, Senegal, Sierra Leone, Togo, and Western Sahara. You soon will find, however, that it is impossible to discuss West Africa completely without taking into account some of the important people groups, religions, languages, commercial influences, and historical events that have overlapped many nations, including countries outside our defined area. Accordingly, many photographs in this text feature places like Cameroon and Chad.

FROM DESERT TO JUNGLE

The land and climate of West Africa change dramatically from the northern Sahara and sub-Sahara zones down to the lower coast of the "bulge." Essentially, the geography is as follows.

From the Atlantic shore of Mauritania eastward through Mali and Niger is a dry, hot, semi-desert area known as the "western Sudan." "The Sudan" is the wide buffer region that spans the African continent just below the Sahara Desert, from the Atlantic Ocean across to the Republic of the Sudan, a large nation on the Red Sea. The northern fringe of the western Sudan receives less than ten inches of rainfall each year.

As we travel south, we enter grasslands called "savannas," where much more rainfall—about fifty inches a year—supports a variety of plant and animal life. The region is at nature's mercy, however. An estimated 100,000 people died, for example, as a result of area droughts in the 1970s and 1980s. During

Agadez, Niger, c. 1926. *Agadez, in central Niger, is a market town some 460 miles northeast of Niamey, the national capital. The town remains the center for the Tuareg, Berber-speaking nomads who wander over the arid plateau. The average rainfall is less than ten inches. Niger is a landlocked western Africa country. Famine and drought are two themes running through its history.*

In 1899 the French began their conquest—which the native population strenuously resisted. Independence was achieved in 1960. Since the 1970s, uranium discoveries have raised hopes for the future. But drought, overpopulation, and political instability have made Niger a poor dependent nation. More than half of its 10 million population are under 15 years of age.

these crises, as much as sixty miles of buffer land along the northern edge of the western Sudan became part of the expanding Sahara Desert.

Below the western Sudan, as we approach the equator and the lower seacoast of the "bulge," lies a stretch of lush forest-land. This green region is more than 100 miles wide between the Gulf of Guinea and the sub-Sahara.

As you would expect, most of the region's people live in the coastal zone. But river basins also provide life-sustaining terrain in the interior. Major rivers of West Africa are the Niger, Volta, and Senegal.

Agadez, Niger, 1926–1927. *This photograph was taken from the top of a sixteenth-century mosque, looking northward. The sultan's palace is in the foreground, and the fort can be seen in the distance. In 2000, the town had only 20,000 inhabitants who live in sand-brick houses that blend in with the countryside.*

The Niger—object of Mungo Park's ill-fated explorations—is the region's longest: 2,600 miles. Africa is a land of mighty rivers, and the Niger is among the most important, ranking third in length behind the Nile and Congo. It begins in Guinea just 150 miles from the continent's west coast and makes a sweeping arc through West Africa. It first flows north-northeastward through the heartland, touches the Sahara Desert, then rolls eastward. It passes a series of large lakes and the legendary city of Timbuktu. At some places it rushes through deep, narrow gorges where navigation is thwarted at low water; at others it spreads to a shallow, gentle expanse six miles wide. By the time it splits into a 200-mile-wide configuration of channels at its delta in Nigeria at the Gulf of Guinea, it has lapped the banks of five countries. Practically every basic geographic and wildlife pattern in West Africa, from savanna to desert to rain forest, can be found along or near the Niger.

A number of significant rivers merge into the Niger: the Mafou, Niandan, Milo, Bani, Kaduna, Benue, and others. Obviously, the Niger basin with its tributaries is vital to life in West Africa. It provides irrigation and hydroelectric power. Ships can ply the lower river for about 200 miles into the interior of Nigeria most of the year, and smaller commercial vessels use most of the upper Niger waterways. Important river ports include Koulikoro, Timbuktu, and Gao in Mali and Baro, Lokoja, and Onitsha in Nigeria. Catfish, perch, and other fish are important food sources. Animal life drawn to the waters vary from hippopotami and other large game to millions of birds, both common and exotic, to the types of creatures that caused sensation and alarm in Europe when the early explorers published their journals: crocodiles, premordial lizards, and dangerous snakes.

Not far from the headwaters of the Niger, the River Senegal begins in the Guinea and Mali highlands and flows 1,020 miles northwestward to the Atlantic coast. For half its length it skirts the border between Senegal and Mauritania. Small villages—usually populated by several hundred people—are found along the Senegal. Some of them farm millet, rice, sugar cane, and other crops. Others are nomadic herders.

The river provided European traders with important access to West Africa during the sixteenth to twentieth centuries. A railway in the 1920s took over the bulk of commercial traffic between the Senegal seaport of Dakar and the interior. The river still is used for inland transportation and commerce, though.

In the lower part of the "bulge," the 1,000-mile River Volta flows southward, watering the nations of Ghana and Burkina Faso. In 1965, the Akosombo Dam was completed to form Lake Volta—one of Africa's major reservoirs, 250 miles long. More than 700 tribal villages were displaced by the lake, but it offers several important benefits: hydroelectric power, a strong fishing industry, and an easy-to-navigate transportation artery between Ghana's seaports and interior.

The Lake Volta project in a way symbolizes the dilemma that confronts much of Africa as a result of European colonization followed by independence. The Europeans insisted they were

Emir of Garoua, Cameroon, 1930. *Garoua, in southeastern Cameroon, is on the Benue River, the longest tributary of the Niger. The town was founded by Modibbo Adama, the Fulani emir who established the Adamawa (Fumbina) kingdom during the first half of the nineteenth century. Eventually, Fumbina extended over present-day eastern Nigeria and most of northern Cameroon as the eastern emirate of the Fulani empire. The emir photographed here is a direct line descendent of Modibbo Adama.*

helping make Africa part of the "modern world." For the last half century, the natives have been counting the costs.

MEDIEVAL KINGDOMS CONNECT WITH THE OUTSIDE WORLD

Primitive tribes probably lived in West Africa tens of thousands of years ago. But it was not until the Arabs arrived in the region, about A.D. 1000, that written records were begun. Arab

Railway. *Typical of railways built in West Africa in the 1920s is this one, in Half Assini in the Gold Coast (now Ghana). The Gold Coast section of the Gulf of Guinea was so called because it was an important source of gold. An area of intense colonial rivalry from the seventeenth century, it was acquired by Great Britain in the nineteenth century. The Gold Coast colony (as Ghana) became a dominion of the British Commonwealth in 1957 and achieved independence in 1960.*

historians described remarkably advanced civilizations already in place, with sophisticated trade networks and farms.

While the people of the region lived in tribes, they also were united at certain periods under great kingdoms. Historians regard these essentially as "merchant empires."

The first great empire of the western Sudan was Ghana. It flourished from A.D. 700 to 1200—not in modern-day Ghana on the lower coast, but north of the Niger and Senegal rivers in

Great Mosque, Jenne, Mali, c. 1887–1889. *The Great Mosque of Jenne was built in the fourteenth century on an island in the Bani River, a tributary of the Niger. It is still in use today and it is the center for Muslim scholarship in southern Mali. Mali rulers adopted Islam during the thirteenth century. As part of French West Africa from 1898 to its independence in 1960, Mali was known as French Sudan. Today about 90 percent of this landlocked state are Muslims.*

what are now parts of Mali and Mauritania. In ancient Ghana, two cultures coexisted in relative harmony: Moslems of Arab persuasion and native blacks, whom the Arabs regarded as pagans because they worshiped ancestral idols.

Invaders, most notably from the south, fractured the Ghana empire around A.D. 1200. Rising in its place was the much larger Mali kingdom, which encompassed both sides of the two great rivers and spread into the lower Sahara Desert.

During the next several centuries, the Mali empire became dominated and exceeded by the Songhai people. Their capital was Gao, a port on the middle Niger. Logically, the Songhai kingdom spread down the river and extended far eastward, covering much of modern Niger.

From the arrival of the Arabs and the formation of the Ghana empire until modern times, camel caravans have plied the Sahara Desert. They have transported goods between West Africa and the Mediterranean (and, via Egypt and the Sinai Peninsula, Arabia). Merchants brought salt and other goods from the north and east, trading them for gold, diamonds and other gems. They also took from Africa natural riches like ivory tusks, pepper, and gum arabic, a substance drawn from acacia trees and used in medicines and certain types of food preparation.

These Saharan traders were a sturdy lot. They also were true "navigators," in every sense of the word. They would set out in their caravans with provisions to last six months. Since they would plod over the hot dunes for days and weeks at a time with no sight of a village or landmark, they had to be able to find their way by skill, just like mariners. An early Spanish traveler in West Africa marveled that these merchants "travel in the desert as it were upon the sea, having guides to pilot them by the stars or rocks."

During the 1400s, European merchants and explorers began sailing south in their little ships. In addition to the difficult desert routes, European-African trade now could be conducted by sea.

Naturally, the first European strongholds on the African continent were built along the coast. Portuguese fortresses had been built in the Gulf of Guinea by the 1470s. Spanish, French, English, and Dutch seafarers soon appeared over the horizon.

Establishing coastal trading posts was no simple matter. The Europeans found few safe harbors along the smooth coast of the continent's "bulge." They were daunted, too, by constant northerly winds. Skirting down the coastline with the wind was fast and simple, but tacking back home into the stiff northerlies was a challenge. Tearful and tense were the partings at European docks in the fifteenth and sixteenth centuries. Sailors' families knew their fathers and brothers might not return.

Elmina Castle, Ghana, c. 1883–1884. *To preserve its monopoly on the Gold Coast trade, Portugal initiated the construction of huge stone fortresses along the coast on sites leased from native chiefs. Elmina Castle, dating from 1482, was the first. In subsequent years, this was supplemented by forts at Axim, Shama, and Accra. The purpose of these forts and their military garrisons was to ensure that the local people sold their gold to agents of the Portuguese king. No other European nation succeeded in establishing a lasting foothold on the Gold Coast before the end of the sixteenth century.*

The Portuguese achieved their goal. Surviving records suggest that up to about 1550, the Portuguese purchased on average at least 12,400 ounces of gold each year, a sizable proportion of the gold then available in Europe from other sources.

Subsequently, the fortress along the Gold Coast passed to the Dutch and the English. They became holding places for slaves during the lucrative slave trade with the American colonies and later with the southern slave states (seventeenth to early-nineteenth century).

Today, Elmina Castle is a tourist site. Its white painted walls stand against a beautiful coastal background. It is a museum, a grim reminder of its slave-holding days. Within the castle, there is a "point of no return," the last door through which the hapless person passed before being forced aboard the slave ship.

Slavery

The earliest traders from the Middle East and Europe risked the long, dangerous journeys to West Africa to obtain the region's natural resources—most desirably, gold. By the 1600s, though, they were trading for a more plentiful item, also of great monetary value: human slaves.

Slavery was common in many parts of Africa among feuding tribes. As African merchants realized there was a great demand for human labor in foreign lands, they aggressively developed the slave trade. Raiding expeditions swept through the interior, carrying away thousands of able-bodied men, women, and children from their villages. They marched their captives to outposts on the coast or to rendezvous with northern camel merchants.

Other slaves were warriors taken captive in battle. Some were travelers who wandered into the villages of slave-trading tribes. Tragically, by the 1700s, slaves were Africa's leading exports.

At first, the Portuguese transported a few slaves to Europe and to their sugar plantations in the nearby Cape Verde and other islands. When the Europeans began establishing colonies in the Americas during the 1500s, African slaves were taken across the Atlantic, first to the Caribbean islands and Cuba, then to mainland North America. A steady stream of ships appeared off the West African coast with one trading objective in mind: human laborers. In exchange, they offered the African chiefs and slave merchants colorful cloth, trinkets, and firearms.

G. K. French, a journalist who chronicled the West African coastal tribes for *National Geographic* in the late 1890s, surmised,

> The white slaver came here for his merchandise, the black slave-owner ashore supplied the trade, and if his barracoons [prison barracks designed to hold slaves awaiting transportation] were empty when a cargo was needed, a quantity of trade goods—rum, gin, cloth, and trinkets— accomplished his purpose in a moment. It was in very truth a survival of the stronger, and one native was as eager to sell his brother as he was to collect his pay from the native procurer.

Cocoa Farm, Ghana, c. 1930. *Ghana is situated on the coast of the Gulf of Guinea. Although relatively small in area and population, Ghana is one of Africa's leading countries because of its natural wealth. It was the first black African country south of the Sahara to achieve independence from colonial rule (1957). Beginning in 1471, with the arrival of Portuguese seamen, Europe's main interest in Ghana was as a source of gold—and later slaves. Both were readily available along the coast in exchange for cloth, metals, arms, and ammunition. The gold industry has an unbroken history dating from the fifteenth century; manganese dating from 1915; diamonds from 1919; and oil from 1970.*

In 1872 Great Britain declared the Gold Coast a British colony—and by 1901 the British had conquered the Asante peoples of the interior. For the next fifty-six years Britain attempted to form one state out of the many tribes. By the 1920s Ghana was producing more than half of the world's supply of cocoa bean; the growing of this commodity probably drew together Ghana's various sections and peoples. Today more than one half of Ghana's arable land is devoted to the cocoa bean, and cocoa provides about 70 percent of the total revenue from exports. This photograph shows ripe cocoa pods being chopped off from the tree, which grows between ten to forty feet tall. The fruit develops into elliptical pods about eight to twelve inches in length. Each pod yields about twenty to forty seeds of cocoa bean. It is from these beans that powdered cocoa and chocolate are made.

An estimated 10–15 million African slaves, perhaps more, were shipped to the New World during the 350-year period ending in the mid-1800s. About two thirds went to Caribbean and South American sugar plantations; Brazil apparently had more slaves than any other New World country. Others went to North America.

Slaves were treated horribly. Some perished before they ever left home, during the violent raids by their countrymen or the torturous journeys to the trading centers. Historians believe about one in five died during the ocean voyage, chained in cramped quarters in the lower decks, ill-fed, suffering from diseases and injuries caused by constant confinement. To those who arrived in the New World, life under many of the plantation overseers was harsh and heartless.

The Coming Clash

By 1800 slavery was being condemned increasingly in Europe and America. Protestant churches led the opposition to slavery, decrying its immorality and cruelty. Finally yielding to this pressure, England outlawed slavery and slave trading in 1807. The Royal Navy even posted warships off the West African coast to chase down slave ships, liberate the prisoners, and bring the slave captains to justice.

The end of the slave-trading era did not bring an end to European interest in Africa, though. By the mid-1800s, foreign merchants and investors saw Africa as a limitless source of untold riches. Here, waiting to be harvested, were priceless ores and gems; exotic timbers; ivory, furs, and other animal products. Foreign traders well knew the promise of such resources along the coast; they could only dream how much more might be found inland. By the 1880s European entrepreneurs were arriving in force.

They found a land ripe for the taking. Tribal kingdoms that had prospered from the slave trade were now weakened and unsure of how to reshape their relationships with the Europeans.

Until the 1800s West Africa had been a place of amazing wonders, beauty, dangers, and change—but general contentment. Olaudah Equiiano, a native Nigerian, explained in 1789,

Musicians, Ghana, c. 1890. *These Ghanaian musicians are playing the xylophone—a set of gradu-ated, tuned wooden bars supported at its nonvibrating points and struck with padded mallets. It is among the most common of African musical instruments.*

[O]ur wants are few, and easily supplied. . . . We have plenty of Indian corn, and vast quantities of cotton and tobacco. Our pine apples grow without culture. . . . We have also spices of different kinds, particularly pepper; and a variety of delicious fruits which I have never seen in Europe. . . . Agriculture is our chief employment, and every one, even the children and women, are engaged in it. Thus we are all habituated to labour from our earliest years.

Everyone contributes something to the common stock; and, as we are unacquainted with idleness, we have no beggars.

Well into the Europeans' colonial years, this state of affairs continued among many West African tribes. Journalist P.A. Talbot wrote of the native Ekoi people in 1912:

> The Ekoi, of extreme southern Nigeria, on the Equator, should be, and probably are, among the happiest people on earth, for they have no taxes to pay, no wearisome restrictions to undergo, and so fruitful is the land that a few weeks' labor is enough to supply them with food, home, and clothes for a whole year.

Under the colonial system, though, disruption of the old ways of life—traditional farming, hunting, building, rituals, music, dance, and so on—was inevitable, and the Africans were in no way prepared. They could not drive the heavily armed invaders away with spears and arrows. After the Europeans took control, natives would be thrust into an industrialized world they did not understand. Then, three generations later, left to govern themselves, they would find themselves in limbo, caught between their ancient way of life and the appalling international demands and pressures of the late twentieth century.

Divo, Ivory Coast, c. 1887–1889. *This photograph is of Divo, south-central Ivory Coast. Today, the town is the chief collecting center for bananas, pineapples, coffee, cocoa, timber, and rubber grown in the surrounding area. Population (2000 est) is 38,000. This photograph was taken by Captain Louis-Gustave Binger, first governor of the French Ivory Coast (1893). In 1899 the Royal Geographical Society honored Captain Binger with its Founder's Medal for his explorations of the Niger River.*

2

"SCRAMBLING" THE LAND

We think of the infamous "scramble for Africa" as something that occurred during the ten or twenty years at the end of the nineteenth century. In a way, it had been going on since the first trading companies arrived on the African coast. White entrepreneurs had worked out exclusive trading rights with native chiefs. Their governments had backed up their claims with force, when necessary. By and large, the coastal tribes had welcomed them and maintained efficient trading posts.

The "scramble" commenced in earnest after a conference of the fifteen European powers in the winter of 1884–1885. The historic West Africa Conference was held in Berlin at the request of Otto von Bismarck, chancellor and prince of Prussia (Germany). Bismarck realized that if Africa was to be colonized without major warfare between the industrialized nations who were contending for the same territories, it must be partitioned diplomatically.

Of course, Bismarck and his contemporaries denied any attempt to divide and conquer the continent. European nations, Bismarck proclaimed, simply should agree among themselves to an orderly way to "help" Africans join the industrial world community.

Many scholars refer to the West Africa Conference as a "carving up" of the great continent. In reality, no formal colonies were established in Berlin. The conference produced a signed agreement, however, whereby the Europeans recognized certain trade domains. They agreed that if a foreign power wanted to claim authority over any African territory, it must formally declare its intentions to other nations—and it must be able to show that it actually held control over the area.

During the next fifteen years, the European powers set about to do exactly that. French, British, and other forces raced to be first to subdue native tribes in key regions. The African continent was transformed from native rule to almost total European administration.

The Europeans had the necessary means, at that point in history, to effect such a conquest. Steam-powered transportation had been perfected. This meant they could bring soldiers, settlers, and industrial equipment to the continent en masse. They could transfer armies quickly along the coast. Deadly firepower was at their disposal—repeating guns and heavy cannons.

To effect their conquests, the Europeans often violated the treaties their traders previously had arranged with the natives. Since the early arrival of European merchants, the whites had fought to secure trading rights with tribes in specific coastal areas of Africa. Sometimes they were able to win treaties with the chiefs—treaties that invariably gave Europeans the keys to the interior in exchange for little of value. When the Europeans encountered tribal resistance to their ambitions, they used force.

One example of how it came about: French officials in the Ivory Coast once paid tribute to certain chiefs in exchange for trading privileges. The natives helped transport goods between the coast and the interior, and the French promised to stay out of tribal affairs. By 1890, though, the French were demanding forced native labor for their expansion projects and were trying to manipulate tribal leadership. In 1900 they instituted a tax on all the natives in the territory. A few years later, they commandeered massive slave labor to build a railroad. So now, rather than paying taxes to the chiefs in exchange for trading rights and services as before, the French still were claiming their old privileges—and more—while ordering the natives to pay *them* taxes.

"Scrambling the Land"

In the Ivory Coast scenario, as we'll see in a later chapter, French heavy-handedness led to native rebellion that would last almost thirty years.

The "Scramble" in the "Bulge"

In the "bulge" of the continent, early European-African trading arrangements had been replaced by the late 1800s. Except in Portuguese Guinea (today's Guinea-Bissau) and Cape Verde, gone from West Africa were the Portuguese and Dutch influences of the sixteenth to eighteenth centuries. Now the dominant European power was France—with an ongoing challenge from England. Bismarck's Prussia controlled one thin strip of land, Togo. (Prussia was more interested in winning other parts of Africa.)

France based its West African initiative in Senegal. Its forces pressed inland along the River Senegal to the Niger and beyond. By 1895 France was "administering" eight general territories in a vast league that became known to the world as French West Africa. After a series of transformations, mergers, and additions during the next few decades, the territories included Dahomey (later to become Benin), French Guinea (today simply called Guinea), French Sudan (Mali), the Ivory Coast (Côte d'Ivoire), Mauritania, Niger, Senegal, and Upper Volta (Haute-Volta—modern-day Burkina Faso).

French West Africa spanned almost 2 million square miles—a seventh of the continent. The capital of this combined domain was Dakar, on the Senegal coast.

The French had arrived in force here after King Louis XIII in 1624 had chartered a trading venture in Senegal. Soon, the French had established a fortress outpost at the mouth of the River Senegal (now the port of St. Louis, on the border with Mauritania). It wasn't until 1815, though, that England, after two centuries of struggle, ended its challenge for control of area trade and recognized French "rights" there.

After the 1884–1885 conference, France spread its claim far into the interior to encompass the regions just described. It placed a governor-general in Dakar to rule its West African domain.

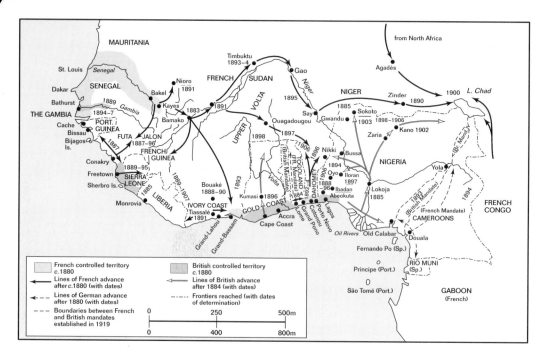

The European Advance into West Africa, c. 1880–1919.

France also claimed the countries of Morocco, Algeria, and Tunisia—most of the western Sahara Desert along the Mediterranean coast. A look at a West African map shows quickly that only a few fragmented pieces of the "bulge" remained for other European powers.

British interests in West Africa by the 1880s were focused in the Niger basin. England had established trading posts well into the interior of present-day Nigeria. At about the time of the West Africa Conference, Sir George Goldie was establishing an English trading empire along the lower Niger. Soon, his Royal Niger Company would give England undisputed claim of Nigeria—one of Africa's largest countries and, to the Europeans, one of the most important.

To the west, separated from Nigeria by French Dahomey (now Benin) and German Togoland, lay the Gold Coast. England exerted control over the coastal part of this territory (modern-day Ghana) in the 1870s. By 1900 the British in the Gold Coast

Colonial Residents, Accra, Ghana, c. 1890. *Accra, the capital and largest city in Ghana, is situated on the Gulf of Guinea (Atlantic Ocean). Since the 1470s, Accra has been a major trading center. In 1877 it became the capital of the British Gold Coast. This photograph was taken by Richard Austin Freeman (1862–1943), a British medical doctor who lived in Ghana for many years. Freeman was a pioneer in the eradication of yellow fever in Ghana. Eventually forced by ill health to retire from medical research, Freeman began to write fiction. He subsequently became a leading author of popular novels and short stories featuring the fictional character John Thorndyke, a pathologist-detective. In the 1970s many of his stories were made into a television serial.*

had expanded their influence by defeating the native Asante kingdom inland.

Elsewhere along the coast of the "bulge," England's control was unchallenged in Sierra Leone, where it had established a colony of former slaves in 1787. Sierra Leone had been a formal British colony since 1808. Several hundred miles to the north, England had established another colony, Bathurst, at the mouth of the River Gambia. Thus, England asserted claim to what became the tiny country of Gambia.

Natives with Barrel of Rubber, Cameroon, c. 1916. *This photograph was taken in Kribi, an Atlantic port in southwestern Cameroon. Rubber, tea, and bananas are grown in the tropical rain forest region. In 1884 Germany claimed this West African area. It established large plantations to grow tropical produce for export. The forced labor system was harsh and cruel for the native population. After World War I (1914–1918), the League of Nations mandate system (1922) (later United Nations trusts) partitioned the area into French Cameroun and British Cameroons. However, the old plantation system was just reorganized under the Cameroon Development Corporation. This corporation became the mainstay of the economy as it provided raw material for European industries while the Cameroons remained dependent on European imported goods. This unbalanced economy continues to plague Cameroon. In a 1961 United Nations plebiscite, the northern part of the British trust voted for union with Nigeria while the southern part joined French Cameroun to become the Republic of Cameroon.*

Germany, meanwhile, was strengthening its grip on sizeable Kamerun (Cameroon), Nigeria's neighbor to the east and south. To the west, on the lower coast of the "bulge," Germany held sway over Togoland.

Portugal, as noted, still held fast to Portuguese Guinea (modern-day Guinea-Bissau) and the Cape Verde Islands. Spain, interestingly, held but one territory in Africa: Spanish (Western) Sahara. Spaniards had claimed that area in the six-

Native Hut, Cameroon, c. 1916. *This photograph was taken in Duala, a Bantu-speaking area of the forest region of southern Cameroon. By the early 1800s, the Duala controlled Cameroon's trade with Europeans. The photograph is of a typical Duala house made from bamboo, a plant that grows extremely high in this area. Its straight stalks are lashed with wooden strips to produce rectangular houses with peaked, thatched roofs.*

teenth century but had been driven out by neighboring Moroccans. In 1884, just before the Berlin Conference set forth its African guidelines, Spain retook the colony, establishing a lonely coastal toehold at the western fringe of the great desert.

It's interesting that although France claimed the lion's share of the territory, England was faring much better in trade operations. By 1880 French trade in West Africa—based along the River Senegal—was valued at an estimated $8 million a year. Meanwhile, British merchants based around the lower Niger were trading three times as much.

THE EUROPEAN VIEW OF AFRICANS

Between the West Africa Conference and the first years of the twentieth century, France and England jockeyed for position in West Africa. In retrospect, their objectives were simple enough: establish sovereignty over Africa's most economically important regions. At the time, though, the European powers claimed to have a broader, nobler mission. They fancied themselves as promoters of a more perfect world. Africa was, among other things, a land to be explored and catalogued in the history books.

Dr. Charles Rabot, editor of the Parisian geographical society's magazine, *La Géographie,* wrote in 1902, "In order to establish beyond dispute her sovereignty over the *hinterland* of her [African] colonies, France has been directing a number of military and civil expeditions whose results have greatly enriched our geographical knowledge of the northern half of the continent." [Rabot, p. 119]

To the Europeans, the Africans were backward, even barbaric. Describing the experience of a French expedition into the "hinterland" of the Ivory Coast and French Guinea in 1899–1900 during which the expedition endured prolonged attacks by native warriors, Rabot wrote,

> All the people inhabiting this part of the tropical forest are cannibals, but they are nevertheless much more civilized than their neighbors; they weave cloth; their villages are quite substantial; their roads are well planned, and they cultivate many vegetables. They hunt men in the Sudan and capture all they can; their captives are then butchered and eaten. . . . When they kill a man, each, according to his rank, receives a special portion; one has a right to the shoulder, another to the thigh, a third to arm and liver. . . . [T]he region will soon be occupied by military French posts, who will try to put an end to these horrible practices.

Some tribal activities were barbaric, without question. The French and their European rivals, though, were not in Africa primarily to "put an end to these horrible practices."

SUBDUING THE NATIVES

By 1900 most of the major European military campaigns to establish control in West Africa had been completed. One of the last struggles took place in the interior of the Gold Coast (today's Ghana). There, the British held a fragile grasp but were threatened by the Germans in neighboring Togo and by the French to the west and north. They also were unnerved by a resurgence of the old native Asante empire under Chief Agyeman Prempe. During the 1890s Prempe managed, by warfare and diplomacy, to reunite divided Asante states. He challenged England's bid to bring Asante lands under British "protection."

The British responded by kidnapping Prempe in 1896 and exiling him to Sierra Leone. During the next several years, they were faced with armed rebellion as they wielded their authority over Asante territory.

Scattered resistance continued in other areas of West Africa well into the colonial era. The French had to contend with tribal rebellions in the Ivory Coast forestlands until the end of World War I in 1918. Their foes were not warriors of one great native kingdom, but a number of small units who periodically harassed the foreign settlements and severed lines of communication in different quarters.

This kind of resistance the Europeans found difficult to subdue. The European style of warfare was one large army pitted against another; the one with the most firepower and/or the wisest commanders usually won. Here the French were faced with no large army against which to aim their devastating artillery. Instead, they were badgered by early guerilla warfare. The natives would appear with little or no warning, strike quickly, and disappear into the bush.

During the 1890s and early 1900s, the bold Ivory Coast rebels pushed French settlers from the interior and kept them confined to coastal ports. That situation changed after 1908. The French administration began to systematically destroy the small African villages and force the tribes to live together in larger towns—where colonial soldiers could keep watch on their activities. In one area, some 150 tribes were consolidated

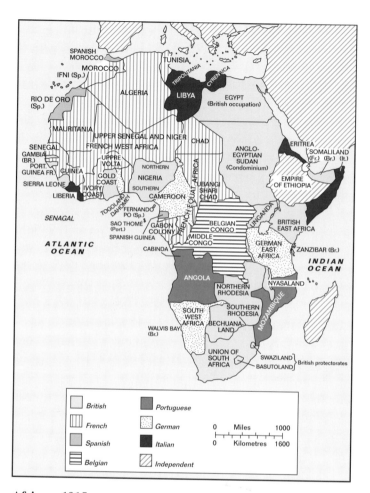

Africa c. 1915.

into ten towns. Gradually, the French confiscated tens of thousands of guns from native warriors, levied heavy fines against resisting tribes, and sent more than 200 native leaders into exile.

The French instituted more policies that angered the blacks. For example, when World War I began in 1914, France pressed an estimated 150,000 colonial subjects into service, most of them West Africans. Shipped to Europe to fight against Germany, some 30,000 natives died. In the Ivory Coast, this event renewed the long-burning fire of resentment among the natives. An uprising in 1916 seriously threatened the French regime in that colony. Unhappily for the blacks, its ultimate failure broke the tribal spirit of rebellion. Since neither their chiefs nor their religious priests had been able to lead the tribes to freedom from French authority, the blacks essentially gave up the fight.

Meanwhile, visionaries like Englishman Frederick J.D. Lugard forged and stabilized the colonies. The story of Lugard in the Niger region is an especially interesting study. An army officer with a distinguished record in various parts of the British Empire, he was engaged by the Royal Niger Company in 1894 to explore and develop British trade along the Middle Niger. All across sub-Saharan Africa, the British were clamoring to beat the French to commercially valuable regions of Africa, and the Niger was considered a major prize.

Lugard's task was formidable. There were natural hazards as well as threats from hostile forces. At one point he was wounded by a tribesman's poisoned arrow, but he survived and eventually succeeded in making the Royal Niger Company a powerful entity on the Dark Continent.

Soon the British government appointed Lugard to form the West African Frontier Force, a regiment of native soldiers commanded by British officers. Its mission was to thwart French progress in the region of the lower and middle Niger. Then, recognizing his success at organizing and managing British interests in Africa, both military and civilian, the government made Lugard the British high commissioner of Northern Nigeria.

Lugard ruled the territory by asserting overall British power in strategic measure, but leaving local government to the natives. He understood the classic, delicate balance required when a minority group—the British—tried to master a huge majority—the natives. The trick was for the colonial administration to support the authority of the tribal chiefs, as long as they ruled within the bounds of Britain's objectives. The British, Lugard knew, should interfere in the people's lives as little as possible.

In 1907 Lugard became governor of Hong Kong. He returned to the Niger in 1912, charged with the role of uniting northern and southern Nigeria. The people of the two regions were—and remain—quite diverse. Probably the greatest achievement of Lugard's long service in the British colonies was the merger of Nigeria at the beginning of 1914. The union was fragile (and continued friction would lead to civil war in Nigeria in the 1960s), so Lugard wisely let the two regions retain their separate identities as far as possible. It was the beginning of modern Nigeria, and Lugard's policy of cooperative rule with native chiefs became the standard modus operandi of British colonial administrations.

After Germany was defeated in World War I, its foreign territories were taken from it and divided by the League of Nations. In West Africa, its Togoland colony was divided between England and France. The western area later became part of the British-held Gold Coast (Ghana). The remainder became another component of French West Africa.

CAREFULLY CRAFTING A PANDORA'S BOX

Critical historians have observed that in "partitioning" Africa, the Europeans set the stage for internal strife that would hamper peace and progress to the present day. Foreign diplomats drew African colonial boundaries to suit their own countries' purposes, not to satisfy any interests of the natives. Long-united ethnic and religious peoples, like the Ewe along the lower coast of the "bulge," were divided and required to serve different European national objectives. Other tribes who long had been at odds were thrown together.

Observing colonial Africa from his position in Parliament, English statesman Lord Salisbury admitted, "We have been engaged in drawing lines upon maps where no white man's foot has ever trod; we have been giving away mountains and rivers and lakes to each other, hindered only by the slight impediment that we never knew exactly where they were."

The territorial divisions seemed logical to the European powers, but they had sometimes disastrous effects on the natives. It was generally within these unnatural bounds that independent African nations eventually would emerge. The Africans then would have to deal not only with their age-old differences, but with newer cultural, religious, social, and economic conflicts planted among them by insensitive foreigners.

Village, Sierra Leone, c. 1900. *This was a typical village in the interior of Sierra Leone. Each village had about 35 circular huts constructed in a tight cluster around a common open space. The photograph was taken by C. L. Weller, a British "traveling commissioner" appointed to sign trade agreements with native chiefs.*

3

LIFE UNDER COLONIAL RULE

The Europeans had to justify their African presence. Critics abroad—and even within their own countries—openly questioned their motives. The official response was that they were in Africa to "civilize" the natives, bring them into the industrial age, convert them to the Christian faith, and keep the peace between warring tribes. Bismarck emphasized at his 1884–1885 West Africa Conference that Europe was morally obliged to help Africa and was not trying to rule it at all. Others at the conference, like British ambassador Sir Edward Malet, agreed.

Clearly, though, the whites in the colonies never intended to bring the blacks up to the same educational and social status as themselves. Racial segregation was the colonial way of life. Many Europeans regarded the African natives as ignorant heathens and gave them little more respect than domestic animals.

The early colonial administrators who knew better made no effort to correct this misperception. They not only wanted the outside world to believe in European

Railway Sidings and Workmen's Dwellings, Southwestern Ghana, c. 1920. *Colonial authorities sometimes paid chiefs to have their people build rail lines. When Ghana achieved independence in 1960, railroad workers were among the first to form a strong labor organization.*

intellectual and social superiority; they wanted the natives to believe it. In the interests of their home governments, they needed to hold the natives back while pretending to bring them into the industrial era.

Educate the Africans? Not a high priority. If native blacks began to think like Europeans, the white governors knew, they soon would expect equal treatment and a proportionate share of their continent's minerals, farm harvests, and other resources. The Africans' "fair share," of course, would be the lion's share—and then some. This would leave little incentive for foreign countries to maintain their colonial systems at all.

Thus, overall, the European governments treated the natives as subordinates. They sometimes exerted a slave-mastering cruelty, but more often employed a firmly enforced system of manipulation. The idea was to keep the natives essentially happy while getting as much cheap (or free) labor from them as possible. The Europeans did not send armies and civilian administrators to Africa simply to rule. Their purpose was to extract Africa's natural resources and make European governments and entrepreneurs wealthy. To accomplish that, it was necessary to keep the African territories at peace and to use native workers in the fields, mines, and factories.

French and English colonial authorities sometimes paid black Africans for their labor—or at least, they paid the tribal leaders. The wages were meager, however, and the taxes high. By the time the workers had paid their obligations to the government, they had gained very little from their long, grueling days of toil.

In French West Africa, natives were subject to what was called the *corvée* system of labor. Chiefs were required to have their people perform a certain amount of work each year for the colonial government. Often this involved building rail lines from seaports to agricultural or mining centers inland. Little more humane than slavery, this method of forced labor was used in West Africa until after World War II.

French colonial administrators in Africa also demanded that certain villages supply quotas of native products. If the natives resisted, they sometimes were killed or maimed by soldiers.

WEST AFRICA THROUGH CAUCASIAN EYES

Images of forced labor and plundering of native products generally were not part of the overall picture that the world acquired of colonial Africa. Through journal reports, books, and newsreels, whites on the outside saw primarily the enchanting aspects of the continent, along with the hardships imposed by nature in a land hardly suitable for civilized folk. They rarely were told of the hardships imposed by colonial administrations on the natives.

Europeans and Americans marveled at pictures of awesome wild beasts spread across the savannas, framed by snow-peaked mountains in the far distance. They saw white government officials relaxing in the porch shade of thatch-roofed huts, enjoying

White Colonials with Ghanian Native. *Photograph in 1890 by British medical doctor Richard Austin Freeman, who lived in Ghana for many years and helped eradicate yellow fever there.*

fruit served by oddly clad natives, and they wished they were there. They perused snapshots of fishers poling tropical rivers in dug-out canoes and wondered what the catch of the day might be, and how it might taste. They studied photographs of ornately clad tribal kings posing with spears and drums and unknown items who purposes the viewers could only guess. They winced at portraits of natives with long porcupine quills piercing their noses, and wondered how these people could be smiling, apparently unhurt. They were intimidated by tales of screaming, bloodthirsty hordes and cannibal feasts—yet they were intrigued, too.

A writer named Cecil D. Priest in the 1920s visited Timbuktu. The fabled city is situated near the northernmost bend of the River Niger in Mali, at the lower edge of the Sahara Desert.

Priest graphically described the market scene, where "five guttural languages may be heard at the same time" and where traders quibbled over the price of "rancid butter" and "fly-blown meat." He watched nomadic Tuareg women sift flour in the streets and listened to musicians perform on primitive instruments. He drank in the panoramic view of the city from the roof of the French governor's palace and described it all thus:

> From this point of vantage could be seen a wonderful moving picture of Arabs, Moors, and Tuaregs wandering along the narrow streets; camels with riders, camels with loads, and donkeys with packs; pedestrians shuttling along with their sandals clattering against their heels; and here and there the red fez cap of a French tirailleur [sharpshooter]. From the market place rose the shrill voices of women and boys calling out their wares. . . .
>
> At 7 o'clock [that evening] I dined on the roof of a house in the South Fort. It was one of those still African nights, with a bright moon. The chanting of the Arab dancers could be heard in the distance, and the steady beat of the tom-tom went on all night.

About 8,000 natives inhabited Timbuktu then, Priest reported, and only 20 Europeans. He noted that "the French do all they can to make themselves happy and comfortable. There is a good hospital and a fine, hard tennis court. Riding and shooting, with tennis, constitute the only forms of exercise. Polo has not found its way there yet, but will sooner or later, I think."

Once a year, he wrote, the "great salt caravan" arrived in Timbuktu from the expanse of desert to the north. This was a major event for residents of the sandy city in the 1920s, just as it had been for their distant ancestors. Again, he provided a description:

> The French Government protects the salt caravan by sending out 200 camel corps men with Europeans in charge. This strong escort defends this wonderful caravan from the ever-threatening attacks of the marauding Tuaregs and desert tribes.

When the caravan enters Timbuktu a great welcome is given the travelers, and the whole town is *en féte* for several days. The big chiefs from the surrounding districts pay their homage to the commander, and thousands of natives come in and buy their annual supply of salt.

The coming of the caravan is a marvelous sight—some 800 camels laden with salt and hundreds of others ridden by gorgeously robed chiefs, with their various bodyguards, either mounted or on foot. The caravan returns north with rice and grain, brought up by canoe [on the Niger] from the large agricultural districts. . . .

Eleanor de Chételat a decade later accompanied her husband, a French government mapmaker and geologist, to the interior of French Guinea. After a wearying, thirteen-hour journey from the seacoast on "a narrow-gauge, wood-burning train that runs only twice a week," they reached the villages of the Fouta Djallon plateau, some 150 miles inland. There, they traveled overland, accompanied by scores of native bearers and attendants.

The villagers greeted them like royalty. Arriving at Touba near sunset, they received a typical welcome:

The reception committee noisily escorted us to our quarters for the night. A clean, carefully swept hut was ready for us, with some drinking water and eggs in one corner. . . . The chief greeted us almost immediately upon our arrival, gave us chickens, and inquired if we had any further needs. To show what a rich country his was, he also offered us oranges, papayas, and bananas.

The natives were at least as intimidated by the French as the visitors were by the natives. Chételat recalled an incident that occurred while their party was "roughing it" in the bush:

Camped near a shallow stream that evening, we decided to refresh ourselves with a plunge before supper as a variation from the usual "dip and pour" shower. About a dozen of our porters were sitting on the bank when we approached, watching us with interest. My husband, wearing trunks, went into the water first, and then I removed my bathrobe, revealing a green bathing suit. The moment I did so they all rushed away into the forest.

Evidently the sight of me had shocked them. Just why I could not understand, for both sexes among the Bassaris go practically naked except for a few ornaments.

In time, the Africans came to regard Chételat as a powerful physician—to her great discomfort. They asked her to treat everything from minor cuts to intestinal worms to malaria. Often she was unable to help them. She wrote of one heartbreaking incident when she was brought an infant with an alarmingly bloated stomach:

> Its parents had carried it hopefully many miles from a distant village. . . . Of course, I had no idea what it was suffering from, and would not have dared prescribe real medicine for such a small baby in any case. For the sake of the parents, almost as much as for that of the baby, I simply had to try something. I gave it some fruit salts and showed the mother how to dissolve more for future use. I never saw it again, nor do I know whether my ministrations were successful.

Chételat learned to cope with the crude ways of bush life— and even to adapt resourcefully. In one place, she and her servants fashioned an oven from a hollowed-out termite mound. She was reminded of where she was, though, when an unwelcome guest claimed the oven for its home one night: "a large, heavy, black spitting cobra."

A European view of black West Africans along the lower coast was captured in part by George K. French, the journalist quoted earlier, who traveled through the region in the 1890s. He described the Fanti people of the Gold Coast:

> The Fantis are an inoffensive, peace-loving, happyhearted race, who readily succumbed to European aggression, but have been exceedingly loth to accept its civilization and Christianity. In common with other

natives of West Africa, with the exception of the Haussas and the Krumen, the Fanti is shiftless and will work only when it is absolutely necessary. Centuries of life without a want that nature did not lavishly supply have quite spoiled him for the advantages of civilization and its accompanying responsibilities, and it is no easy task to convert him to the ways of European life; yet he is tractable and readily governed, and the colonial official and trader find no great difficulty in utilizing him for many purposes.

Native Africans undoubtedly held a quite different perspective of the alleged "advantages of civilization and its accompanying responsibilities."

French went on to chronicle some of the customs of West Africans that seemed bizarre to westerners:

The stranger visiting the Gold Coast will at first be sorely puzzled by the similarity of the names of the natives. Every child takes its surname from the week-day of its birth, and strangers theirs from the day of their arrival, with an additional sobriquet descriptive of some personal peculiarity. For instance, a child born on Wednesday receives the name of that day of the week, Kwako. Kwabina (Tuesday) and Kwako are held to be "strong days" of birth; but children that appear on Fridays, Saturdays, and Mondays are considered "weak as water." Nothing will induce the Fanti to sleep with his head toward the sea or to take possession of a new dwelling-house on a Tuesday or Friday, both these days being regarded as unlucky for this purpose. . . .

In common with many other natives of Africa, the Fanti lives in close communion with the vague and mysterious beings of the unseen world. A large proportion of his time is spent in consulting or appeasing the deities that inhabit the earth, the air, the sea, the rivers, and even trees, sticks, stones, and bits of cloth. If he is ill, he believes that his ancestors are summoning him, and he at once proceeds to consult the fetichman [keeper of tribal idols, witch doctor]. . . . They bury their dead in their houses, choosing a room that afterward can be kept fastened up or secluded.

This custom the colonial authorities have attempted to abolish on sanitary grounds, but the effort has not wholly succeeded.

Obviously, Priest, Chételat, French and other correspondents held a decidedly "outside" view of Africans, their needs, and their future. French believed that, as he put it, "England's enlightened policy in other parts of Africa will undoubtedly be applied here [the Gold Coast] and will result in the ultimate spread of civilization throughout this darkest part of the dark continent."

European-style civilization indeed spread through many parts of Africa. But it encountered dire complications that French and his colleagues could not have foreseen.

Gospel Light and Enlightenment

Christianity spread substantially through West Africa during the colonial era, except in the long-established Muslim strongholds of the sub-Sahara. A number of Protestant and Catholic missionary societies in Europe raised funds and sent evangelists and teachers to West Africa during the 1800s. Christian blacks in Africa, meanwhile, themselves sponsored missions that reached far inland from their coastal bases.

The best-known Christian evangelist was a Liberian black prophet named William Wade Harris, whose preaching greatly affected natives in the neighboring Ivory Coast. As many as 120,000 followers a year abandoned their ancient gods and built Christian churches. In 1916 the French colonial government banned Harris from their colony because some of his followers, educated in church-run schools, were beginning to fan the flame of African independence.

The Christian church thus played a significant role in West Africa's early politics of independence. Christian missionaries throughout the Europeanization of Africa, beginning with the Portuguese in the 1400s, had accomplished much practical good—operating schools and providing health care for the natives. They also had worked constantly to translate African languages, opening communications between natives and foreigners.

Emir, Cameroon, 1930. *Most probably, this photograph is of a Kanuri emir. The Kanuri have been Muslims since the eleventh century. Today, about one-fifth of the Cameroons are Muslim, and nearly half the population are below age fifteen. More than 200 different ethnic groups live in the Cameroon. There are three main language divisions: the Bantu-speaking south; the Sudanic of the north; and those who speak semi-Bantu in the west.*

The colonial powers were not inclined to develop good government-run schools. Through the first two decades of the twentieth century, only a small fraction of the schools in most West African countries were government-supported. Thus, the responsibility for education, especially during the first half of the colonial period, primarily fell to missionary teachers.

Group of Natives, Gold Coast, c. 1883-1884. *This photograph was taken in the village of Half Assini at the Ghana border with the Ivory Coast. Half Assini's claim to fame is that Kwame Nkrumah (1909–1972), the Ghanaian nationalist leader and the first president of an independent Ghana (1957–1966), was born nearby and spent nine years at a Roman Catholic elementary school in Half Assini. Nkrumah fondly describes the town in his 1957 autobiography. J. Morrow Campbell, the photographer, was a British engineer involved in railroad construction in Ghana.*

To an extent, the missionaries escaped a portion of the resentment that was building among the blacks against the Europeans. Church workers, residents could see, plainly were in Africa to help. They lived among the villagers, conversed in the local languages, and did what they could to improve the lot of the natives. Sometimes, government officials suspected missionaries were *too* helpful. In the early years of colonialism, authorities looked askance at the progress mission schools were making in educating the tribes.

While Europeans in one way or another were making themselves at home all across Africa, a single black country stood independent. In the next chapter, we'll examine the extraordinary story of Liberia.

Sierra Leone, 1900. *The graves at Waima in Konno Country of Sierra Leone.*

4

A Nation Founded on Freedom

They were called "Americo-Liberians," and they were absolutely unique. As we've learned, millions of slaves were kidnapped from West Africa during the sixteenth to nineteenth centuries and shipped in irons to work on plantations in North, South, and Central America and the Caribbean. In 1822 a few of them returned, freed representatives of the American Colonization Society. The winds of abolition were blowing strong in both Europe and America—but what to do with the African slaves after they were freed? Ship them back to Africa, reasoned some abolitionists.

Many repatriated slaves in the United States agreed, but they did not necessarily wish to be absorbed into their ancestral tribes. As they saw it, they had become "Americans," and they were not ashamed of it. In fact, they believed their tribal relatives in Africa should become Americanized. So they founded the small Republic of Liberia on the southwestern angle of the continent's "bulge" and established there an American-style democracy.

The plan seemed outlandish to many observers, both black and white. Even now, historians are amazed by the "Americo-Liberian" experiment—not just because of its drastic purpose . . . but because it basically worked. Liberia remains independent, although it has undergone severe civil strife and bloody political upheavals in the late twentieth century. Unlike every other African country, it never fell under European rule.

FLOCKING TO THE COAST

The American settlers chose a humid but feature-rich locale. Coastal beaches, swamps, and lagoons rise to forested hills and plateaus, with low mountains inland. Liberia is a country of many rivers, year-round greenery, and abundant animal life.

When the Americans began to arrive around 1820, Liberia was populated by native tribes. Along the coast and rivers lived fishers. Inland were subsistence farmers, workers who grew what they needed to supply their families. They grew rice, millet, and sorghum. Some of the descendants of ancient hunter-gatherers still found their livelihoods in the wild, just as area tribes had for many centuries. Through Mandingo merchants, they traded goods with peoples living in other parts of West Africa.

During the late 1400s native tribes had begun trading with the Portuguese who came by ship to explore the coast of the "bulge." This opening of trade by sea lured more people from the African interior to settle near the Liberian coast. Traders from other European countries began arriving at what they called Africa's "Grain Coast." Ironically, grain was not the primary trading commodity taken from the region; rather, the Europeans were interested in a type of pepper, *melegueta,* which they called the "grain of paradise."

Soon the major trading items were not edibles of any type, but human slaves. Not many slaves actually were captured in Liberia. Rather, the Liberian tribes functioned as intermediaries and let the Europeans operate slave trading outposts in the area. The captives came mostly from the interior, transported to the coast by Mandingo, Gola, and other native middlemen.

Slaves Come Home to Freedom

The effort to repatriate freed slaves to their native continent did not begin in Liberia. At neighboring Sierra Leone in 1787 a small group of freed blacks backed by the English parliament set up an independent colony. The port of Freetown in Sierra Leone was where the Royal Navy typically set prisoners ashore when they captured slave ships off the West African coast.

It might be suggested, in fact, that Sierra Leone was where the first rays of pan-African independent thought originated in West Africa—even before the Europeans took over the continent. Christianity quickly thrived in Freetown, to such an extent that black Freetown Christians supported mission projects up and down the West African coast. In 1857 they founded the famous Niger Mission where, under black bishop Samuel Ajayi Crowther, educating the natives was a priority (which unsettled the British regime in Nigeria).

Across the Atlantic, the American Colonization Society (ACS) was organized in 1816. This group included famous leaders like Daniel Webster and Henry Clay and was endorsed by Thomas Jefferson and then-President James Madison. Bushrod Washington, a nephew of George Washington, was the society's first president.

Two reasons motivated the society to return slaves to their homeland: (1) the members realized slaves had been greatly wronged, and they wanted to make amends; and (2) some American abolitionists feared that certain freed slaves, embittered by years of wretched treatment, might pose a threat to white society. ACS agents began looking for a West African locale to establish an intermediate colony—a sort of "camp" where freed slaves could live under self-government until they were ready to rejoin their ancestral tribes.

Eighty-eight freed blacks sailed from New York to West Africa in 1820 in the ship *Elizabeth*. The English refused to let them land at Freetown, so they put ashore farther to the south at Sherbro Island. The settlement failed; many people died from disease, and the rest retreated to Sierra Leone. The next year, however, American representatives negotiated the purchase

Sierra Leone, 1928. Natives pounding oil palms. *Palm oil is used in making soap, candles, and lubricating greases. The oil from the palm kernel is used in such edible products as margarine and chocolate.*

from native Basa chiefs of a strip of land between the Junk and Mesurado rivers. For the equivalent of $300 in trade goods, what would become the nation of Liberia was born. In 1822 settlers established a village near modern-day Monrovia. During the next twenty years, almost 5,000 blacks sailed from America to Liberia.

Vexingly, one of the terms of the land purchase was that the liberated slaves who settled in Liberia would *not* try to disrupt the natives' slave trade—an important source of wealth to the Basa.

A Mindset of Independence

From the outset, the colonists determined they would live free of outside influence. One of their first leaders, Elijah Johnson, declined military protection offered by the English in Sierra Leone when natives attacked the settlers. Johnson knew that if the British lent their protection, they also would "lend" their domination, in short order. The colonists, Johnson asserted, would have to be self-reliant if they were to be self-governing.

The colony was named Liberia, meaning "free land," in 1824. The main settlement was named Monrovia after American President James Monroe, an important supporter of the colony. It expanded, and similar colonies of freed slaves were established along the coast. Two leading colonies in 1838 merged to form the U.S.–aligned Commonwealth of Liberia, and other colonies eventually joined. From its beginning, Liberia was strengthened by military and economic ties to the United States.

In 1847 the settlers voted to replace the commonwealth with a truly self-controlling Republic of Liberia. Its government was patterned after that in America, with a president, senate, house of representatives, and separate judicial branch. Joseph Jenkins Roberts, born in Virginia, was the republic's first president.

Maintaining its independence through the coming century amid Europeanized Africa was not easy. Heavy debt to British banks in the 1860s and 1970s, for example, almost brought the country to its knees and led to the impeachment and imprisonment of Liberian president Edward James Roye. Ups and downs in international markets affected Liberia's economic health. Weakened, the republic was at the mercy of England and France, who annexed much of Liberia's land into their neighboring colonies. By 1911 almost half the territory of the original Liberian republic had been taken over.

Meanwhile the government was having trouble controlling its own native tribes. During the 1870s a union of Grebo chiefs formed a kingdom and declared themselves independent. They considered themselves free to trade with foreigners as they wished, ignoring Liberia's economic policies. A bloody rebellion ensued and was put down only with the help of the U.S. Navy.

The Grebo rebellion symbolized a troublesome core division among the people of Liberia. The government was run by American settlers and their descendants—a tiny minority of the population—who regarded themselves as separate from the natives. Not until the twentieth century did they gradually interact seriously with the old tribes. By the mid-1900s, other African nations were breaking free of the white colonial minorities who had controlled them; oddly, in Liberia, a similar controlling minority of Americo-Liberian blacks still held sway.

President William V.S. Tubman, who took office in 1944 and was reelected an unprecedented five times (he died in office in 1971), made a major effort to end this internal division with his Unification Policy. Among other results, he obtained voting rights for native property holders and taxpayers and developed close ties with tribal chiefs in the interior, or "hinterland." Tubman is remembered as the "Maker of Modern Liberia."

LIBERIA'S PLACE IN INDEPENDENT AFRICA

While many African nations began their independence in the mid-twentieth century plagued by weak and worsening economies, Liberia generally prospered during that period. Since the 1920s it had realized substantial benefits from foreign-owned industries. Firestone Tire and Rubber Company, for example, in 1926 signed a 99-year agreement with the Liberian government to lease a million acres of land for rubber production. Not only did this put needed revenue in the country's coffers, it gave some 20,000 natives jobs with housing, medical, and other benefits. Firestone also built roads, railroads, and communication lines and helped in the country's hydroelectric development.

The country is rich in minerals (especially iron ore) and farmland (50 percent of the country's soil is arable). It is blessed by a favorable climate and sustains both oceanic and inland fishing industries. Not until the late 1970s did depressed

Twisting Raffia for Cloth and Masks, West Africa, 1928. *In western central Africa, the textile industry was based on a fiber drawn from the raffia palm. The fibers were dyed a variety of colors and woven into cloth. Raffia also was used to make ceremonial masks that were decorated with shells, beads, and feathers. The Casamance region of Senegal that lies south of the Gambia along the Casamance River is covered by raffia palms.*

prices drag down its economic growth rate. Then, in the 1990s, the country's farming and industry were hurt by civil war.

Liberia today has more than 2,000 villages. The principal city remains Monrovia, overlooking the Atlantic. Founded in 1822, Monrovia is home to a varied sampling of Liberia's overall population, which includes sixteen ethnic groups.

Most Liberians are Christians. Approximately 15 percent are Muslims, most of whom live in the northwest near the Guinea and Sierra Leone borders. About the same percentage practice traditional black African religious customs.

The Republic of Liberia is unusual not only because of its remarkable past, but because of its relative stability, until recent decades, among the African nations. Few citizens move away, and its population is growing faster than that of most other countries. Public school education is required for those aged six to sixteen, and is free. (About a third of the children, however, do not attend.)

Another interesting feature is the makeup of Liberia's work force. About two thirds of the people work in agriculture—and the majority of agricultural workers are women.

Even more unusual: Although Liberia does not have a prominent maritime economy, it has a higher tonnage of registered ships than any other country in the world. Many ships owned by other countries are registered under Liberia's "flag of convenience," because Liberia's taxes are low.

As you would expect, western lifestyles and influences are especially strong in Liberia. But government institutions and schools are mindful of the people's ethnic diversity and long-held traditions, and promote respect for age-old African culture. Traditional music is heard, particularly in rural communities. Ancient arts like mask making have been handed down to the current generation.

RECENT POLITICAL STRIFE

After Tubman's death in 1971, Liberia entered a quarter-century of economic crises and political unrest, sometimes deadly. William R. Tolbert, Jr., the vice president and an Americo-Liberian like Tubman, became president. Rioting erupted in 1979 because of rising food prices, and Tolbert was killed in a military takeover the next year. Sergeant Samuel K. Doe assumed the presidency and was duly elected to the post in 1985—amid charges of voting corruption. Doe's administration ruthlessly jailed and sometimes killed political rivals.

By 1990 political factions were so incensed that civil war broke out. Doe was killed. After a West African peacekeeping force intervened, the warring forces accepted a cease-fire. Two years later, though, fighting resumed. More than 150,000 people ultimately died, and an estimated half of Liberia's people were uprooted. Not until 1996 did the opposing factions sign a formal peace treaty.

Ruth Perry led a transitional government in 1996—becoming the first woman head of state in post-colonial Africa. In July 1997 a one-time rebel leader, Charles Taylor, was elected president. Initially applauded by key black leaders in the U.S., Taylor recently has been criticized for his government's human rights record.

Tasso Men in Sherbro Island, Sierra Leone, c. 1890 (T. J. Alldridge). *This photograph was taken on Sherbro Island, off the southwestern coast of Sierra Leone. The island, about thirty-two miles long and up to fifteen miles wide, had been acquired in 1861 from the Sherbro people by the British colony at Freetown. The town of Bonthe served as a nineteenth-century British coastal post to control the illegal slave trade. Little exploration of the interior had been done.*

The headdresses of these native men were made from a framework of bones, elaborated with human and animal skulls. The rattles on their legs served to emphasize their movements and to intensify the effect of any ritual dance in which they partook.

This is one of a series of photographs taken by T. J. Alldridge, who was a "traveling commissioner" appointed by Great Britain to negotiate agreements with native chiefs. This policy was instituted in 1888 as a way to deal with internecine wars in the West African interior that were seriously disrupting Britain's lucrative trade in timber and vegetable oils. The trade agreements also served to bring native chiefs into the British sphere of influence.

For almost ten years T. J. Alldridge traveled as one of the commissioners to unmapped regions of Sierra Leone. His photographs of the people and their customs form a remarkable historical record. They are among the first known images of Sierra Leone's interior areas. In 1900 the Royal Geographical Society honored Alldridge for his contribution to ethnography.

5

A GROWING SPIRIT OF INDEPENDENCE

In time, native Africans were bound to embrace a certain principle their European overseers held dear: self-government. Freedom from outside dominion certainly was not a new idea to them. It always had been an objective of African tribes and kingdoms. For centuries, they had fought for control over their domains, large and small. The powerful tribes had earned the right to impose their will; the weak ones had learned to survive in bondage.

But this new arrangement, with colonial powers from abroad exerting control, was different. In the past, neighboring tribes might have had any number of arguable motives to challenge one another's territorial rights. But what rights at all had white Europeans in black Africa? Sooner or later, the question would be dealt with.

Why was it not dealt with when the Europeans first arrived? Why did tribal warriors not drive them out before colonial governments could be established? In part, it was because the whites were shrewd. One result of the peculiar form of joint control they established in colonial Africa, especially in the British colonies, was that many Africans never thought of themselves as "conquered." In the bush, they saw little of the white administrators and soldiers. Daily life and ancient customs and ceremonies went on just as during the times of their ancestors. Even when they felt the effects of European domination, such as taxation, native blacks rather than white strangers carried out most of the policies. Most Africans regarded the port town bureaucrats, the white merchants, and the small garrisons of uniformed soldiers with curiosity—even admiration—rather than animosity. Natives eagerly served under European administrators in various capacities.

True, the Europeans were raping the continent's natural resources (France, for example, increased foreign trade and revenues from French West Africa by more than ten times during the colonial era). But native Africans themselves were deeply involved in the business as middlemen. Certain tribal chiefs became wealthy off the Europeans' ventures. As long as these chiefs kept their people subdued, the colonial regimes had little to fear. Whites and blacks coexisted peacefully for the most part, though segregated.

As the twentieth century progressed, though, the results of colonial oppression became more obvious to all—and the drive for independence became a groundswell.

DIFFERENT "STYLES" OF LONG-RANGE GOVERNMENT

It's important to note that the European powers exercised different forms of administration over their foreign colonies, which in turn affected the general course of independence movements.

Great Britain shrewdly sought to place as much authority as possible in the hands of natives—but with British officials ultimately in control, and with Britain reaping the rewards of commerce from the area. British colonial leaders like Lugard, as we saw earlier, recognized early that they never would be able to fully oversee and police such broad territories with their own nationals. And they hoped that when a colony eventually became independent—as most British leaders knew would happen—London could maintain valuable ties with the new country.

France held a different perspective. It considered its colonies actual extensions of France—"Overseas France." It encouraged settlement in the territories by French nationals who were involved in industry and agriculture. At the same time, it regarded the natives as French subjects—although not equal in status to French nationals. Natives who wanted to be treated as real "French" people were expected to abandon much of their African heritage, speak the French language, and live the way the French lived. Not many natives were interested in doing that. The comparative few who tried found it no small task, especially as the French colonial administrations provided only meager educational facilities.

Moreover, the French were less willing than the English to let the tribes rule themselves in daily matters. While the British forged wary but long-term alliances with important native chiefs, the French fostered such alliances only temporarily. When the French government felt secure in controlling an area, the puppet chief typically was deposed and the French authorities established direct rule over the people.

Sporadic Opposition

Some of the natives (like those who harassed the French in the Ivory Coast from the 1890s through World War II) tried to resist white rule. But the armies of the industrial nations demonstrated that they ultimately could win in warfare. Spear-throwing natives' strength in numbers meant little in the face of machine guns. Unions of warriors were able to ambush or overwhelm European forces on occasion, but they usually suffered horrible carnage in retaliation.

Nevertheless, overtures toward an independent Africa were made even while the continent was being partitioned and colonized. During the 1890s the Aborigines' Rights Protection Society was formed to contest large-scale claims by Europeans to African land and win more administrative jobs for natives in the colonial governments.

The First Pan-African Conference was held in London in 1900, bringing together native Africans and activists of African descent from other nations. They voiced opposition to European colonization, but the conference did little to unite Africans against the invaders. Nor did it significantly affect world opinion about what was going on in Africa.

In retrospect, it almost seems that African colonialism had to "run its course" for a generation or two before a majority of Africans reached the level of discontent that demanded independence.

Mounting Tension

African disdain for European interlopers dated, to some degree, to the years of the first European explorers. It increased steadily during the colonial period.

An issue that fueled much of the greatest resentment during colonial times—resentment that would evolve into a spirit of pan-African independence—was taxation. The European governments taxed Africans on international products that were bought and sold in the colonies. They also taxed the people directly, requiring money or goods from families or villages, or in some areas requiring a certain amount of free labor each year on behalf of the government.

Just as American colonists challenged English "taxation without representation" in the late 1700s, blacks in Africa realized there was no legitimate reason to surrender their meager earnings to colonial governments that did little to improve their welfare. They were especially incensed because white settlers in colonial Africa usually weren't subject to such severe taxation.

World War I sowed fresh seeds of discontent among the natives. For one thing, tens of thousands of black Africans died in Europe, pressed into fighting for a cause they never embraced. For another, those who returned had interacted with free soldiers. As a result, they began to realize how dismal was their comparative lot, living under the thumb of foreign governments, working not to improve their own people's station in life but to make already prosperous foreigners even more prosperous.

A Growing Spirit of Independence

Poro Group, Guarea Area, Sierra Leone, c. 1890 (T. J. Alldrige). *Guarea is grown in the interior of Sierra Leone. This unusual tree is noted for its cedar-scented, pink mahogany-type wood. This* poro, *or secret society, was one of the most characteristic Guinea Coast institutions, especially in areas that lacked a strong government. In Sierra Leone and Liberia, these groups achieved such power that they were crucial during the precolonial period in maintaining law and order. The* poro *developed as the major organization responsible for enforcing traditions and for punishing serious offenses such as incest and murder.*

The poro *educated boys and girls. It also became involved in agricultural practices as well as in military training. Rank in a* poro *group was essential for anyone in an authoritarian position. In 1898 the* poro *of the Mende people organized an unsuccessful uprising against British expansion into the Sierra Leone interior.*

At the close of the war, Africa was ravaged by a flu epidemic. It was apparent to the natives that this strange, deadly disease was spread by the Europeans, for it essentially followed the colonial rail lines through the interior. Thousands of Africans died.

In the mid-1930s, native West Africans again were called on to train and fight in a European-instigated world war. This time, though, their first destination was not the trenches of Europe. Rather, they were transported to the eastern tip of their own

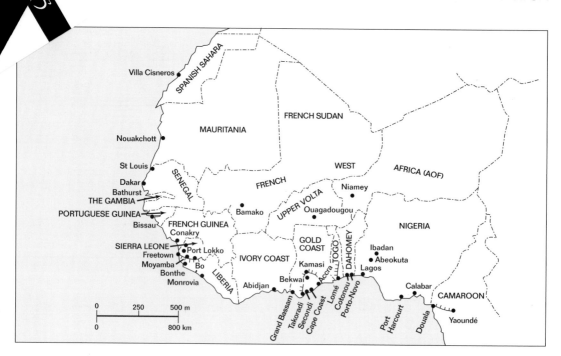

West Africa, 1919–1935.

continent. They were needed to help liberate Ethiopia, which had been overrun by Italian forces. Italy was allied to Germany—France and England's great enemy—as war clouds gathered across Europe. Together, British and other European soldiers fought alongside black battle units from West Africa and elsewhere to drive out the Italians. They saw the native emporer, Haile Selassie, restored to his throne . . . and they took notice when Great Britain recognized Ethiopia as an independent nation.

Throughout World War II, Africans endured combat hazards and hardships for the causes of freedom and self-rule, just as their fellow white soldiers did. Unavoidably, when the blacks returned home after the war, they brought with them a fresh attitude about their place in colonial society, and about their place in the world. After World War II, it was absurd for Europeans to expect the Africans who had fought beside them for freedom to accept a permanent role of servitude in the "free world."

GRADUAL PROGRESS IN EDUCATION

Many Africans received a modest education in colonial schools, and some were given jobs in the public sector. They were service roles, however, not management or policy-making opportunities. Native blacks worked as teachers, police officers, hospital staff, clerks, guides, and interpreters for the government and foreign-owned industries. They easily could be replaced if they caused trouble for the colonial administrators. While they made valuable contributions and could take pride in their work, their subordinate status was obvious to all and caused growing resentment.

Not until the 1920s did the British government in Africa take serious steps to improve the lot of its native subjects. At length, the British were pressured to adopt formal standards for educating the Africans under their charge. The British began providing subsidies to mission schools. Some schools began to include instruction in native languages and other African traditions.

By the end of World War II, real educational progress could be seen—or at least anticipated—in the British colonies. Independent-minded Africans were gaining increased control over their own affairs and were becoming involved in developing their own educational programs. Secondary education was expanded. New universities were founded in major cities across the continent.

The French, meanwhile, implemented formal education policies in French West Africa between 1903 and 1918 and built a number of schools and vocational colleges. Yet, it is estimated that by 1945, only a fraction of 1 percent of the people in French West Africa were enrolled in government-sponsored schools.

It is noteworthy that the French government, in colonial policy statements, asserted that the main purpose of education should be to "expand the influence of the French language, in order to establish the nationality or culture in Africa." Specifically, French African schools were intended for "training an indigenous staff destined to become our assistants throughout the domains, and to assure the ascension of a carefully chosen elite." A second objective was "educating the masses, to bring them nearer to us and to change their way of life."

As in the British colonies, real educational progress in French West Africa began after World War II. Blacks became citizens of the so-called French Union. The University of Dakar—the first university in French West Africa—was established in Senegal. School and college attendance quadrupled between 1945 and 1957 (although it remained dismally low by world standards). Scholarships were made available for native students to continue their studies in France.

Comparatively, education progressed faster after World War II in the British colonies than it did in French West Africa.

Bundu Devil, Sierra Leone, c. 1890 (T. J. Alldridge). *This is a rare photograph of a so-called* bundu *devil. T. J. Alldridge was also able to obtain a very fine specimen of a* bundu *devil mask. It is on permanent display in London's British Museum. Alldridge gives this description (1894) of the person called the* bundu *devil:*

The Bundu devil is a "medicine" woman, who is believed to be capable of casting spells, for good or evil, over the destinies of the men. There is generally a Bundu devil in any large town belonging to an important chief, but she does not appear in her peculiar costume unless she is especially called out to look into some misbehaviour on the part of the men, or upon some gala occasion, or upon the visit of strangers whom it wished to honour. I had myself many opportunities of observing this remarkable personage, who naturally inspires her people with much awe, and commands the greatest respect from all classes.

Her distinctive costume is unvarying. All Bundu devils being similarly attired, except as regards the headpiece, which admits of some slight difference. No part of the body may be visible, consequently the cloth casings of the arms and legs are sewn up at the extremities. In each covered hand the "devil" carries a bunch of twigs, with which she goes through a sort of dumb-show, as she never does any talking. Her dress is of a long shaggy fibre, dyed black, and over her head she wears a grotesque wooden mask. Occasionally she indulges in a dance, but owing to the great heat produced by dancing in so heavy a dress, a little goes a long way, and after a few moments she retires to some quiet part of town, where her attendant, who is always present with a large country mat, unrolls it, and encircles the "devil," who is then able to remove her mask and obtain a little fresh air away from the gaze of the madding crowd. I have had the honour of shaking the covered hand of a good many of these devils . . . The fetish power of these beings is very great.

A decade after the war, only about 340,000 children, or 1.7 percent of the population, were attending French schools. In British-controlled Nigeria, more than 2 million children, or 6 percent of the population, were in school. In Britain's Gold Coast colony, attendance was at almost 600,000, or 12 percent of the population. Meanwhile, the opportunity for a university education was substantially better in Nigeria and the Gold Coast than in the countries of the French Union.

In Portuguese Guinea, colonial leaders by and large left education up to church missions.

THE POLITICS OF INDEPENDENCE

Slowly but surely, a class of educated blacks was growing in both British and French West Africa. Some became doctors and lawyers, some professional journalists. These natives saw no reason why Africans shouldn't be given greater responsibilities in the colonial governments. Ultimately, they saw no reason why Africans shouldn't govern themselves. The Europeans, of course, clearly understood that if the Africans took control of their own national affairs, colonialism on the Dark Continent was doomed.

Deepening bitterness at being held back by colonial governments led to organized political opposition. Miners, farmers, and railroad workers occasionally went on strike. At one point during the 1930s, cocoa growers in the Gold Coast banded together and refused to sell their produce, forcing buyers to improve market prices.

Blacks began forming political parties to campaign for native interests and equality—but not, at first, for independence. One of the early political groups in French West Africa was the Senegalese Socialist Party, organized in Senegal during the 1930s. The African Democratic Rally (RDA), which initially had close ties to the French Communist Party, was founded in 1946. Predictably, the entrenched colonial regimes firmly opposed it. France did, however, agree to let colonial blacks elect ten delegates to the French National Assembly in Paris beginning in 1946.

Poro Man in Sierra Leone, c. 1890 (T. J. Alldridge). *This is a photograph of a poro in full ceremonial outfit. T. J. Alldridge was restrained when he described it as "very peculiar."*

A hoop encircles the waist, from which descends a cascade of fibre reaching to the ankles. A netting of country cotton is over the body; a curious head-dress, not unlike the front of a mitre, and of fantastic device, is usually worn, and some sebbehs, or fetish charms, hang from the neck . . . . When the boys have completed their training and ceremonies in the Poro, they are eligible to attend Poro meetings; and all assemblies and consultations of chiefs upon secret country matters; whether of war, peace, or what not . . . .

The RDA soon severed its association with the communists, and a variety of political parties devised coalitions in French West Africa. Native political groups were by no means united, though, when the government in Paris was restructured in 1958 under Charles de Gaulle and France offered its African colonies the opportunity to govern themselves.

In the British West African colonies, independent political forces were having an undeniable impact on regional affairs by the late 1940s. Kwame Nkrumah, a western-educated native and political activist, organized a nationalist-minded Convention People's Party in the Gold Coast. He led a boycott against European-run businesses. Political riots broke out in several Gold Coast towns. Nkrumah served a short term in prison . . . and emerged more aggressively determined for independence.

Rather than retaliation or punishment, the British wisely if reluctantly responded with a government reorganization that gave blacks substantial control. A new constitution for the Gold Coast in 1951 resulted in a black-dominated ruling assembly, with black leaders placed in positions of administrative authority. Independence for the Gold Coast was in clear view—and other British colonies in Africa were inspired by the Gold Coast to pursue sovereignty for themselves.

These other nations, though, faced a more troubled course toward independence, not because their colonial governments were notably different from that in the Gold Coast, but because of such factors as unpredictable economic situations, differing population concentrations, and deep divisions among their peoples along religious and cultural lines.

For example, Nigeria was dangerously divided between Muslims in the north and native blacks in the south. Two political parties established power in the lower region: the National Convention of Nigerian Citizens (NCNC) in the east and the Action Group (AG) in the west. Although they held different views and pursued different interests along tribal lines, both parties wanted to follow the example of the Gold Coast in forging self-rule. Not so in the north, where Muslims held secure positions in the colonial administration. These aristocratic native leaders, while not firm supporters of the British colonial system, considered colonialism better than an independent Nigeria possibly dominated by NCNC and AG leaders.

So it was across much of Africa. As the Europeans took steps to pull out during the 1950s, a complex assortment of divided factions clamored to fill the coming void in government.

Two Dancers, Sierra Leone, c. 1890 (T. J. Alldridge). *Aldridge described the dancers thus:*

The dancing costume, consists of a netting of country cotton worn over the body, long bushy branches of palm-leaf fibre suspended from the thickly plaited bangles of the same fibre round the arms and wrists, various sebbehs *or* gree-gree *charms hanging from the neck, and short knicker-bockers of country cloth tied above the knees by palm-leaf string, to which are fastened small pieces of hollow iron, with little rings loosely hanging from them, which as the dancing goes on, jingle not unpleasantly, for native iron gives out a somewhat rich sound. The chief feature in the get-up is, however the "dressing" of the girls' faces; which means that these faces are covered with strange devices, produced by the smearing on with the finger of a substance called* wojeh, *composed of white clay and animal fat. The coiffure is a high and mostly elaborated super-structure, worked in small patterns—a very favorite design, closely resembling that curious concretion known to geologists as the brain-stone—and embellished by a silver* gre-gre, *or by a bunch of seeds.*

Today, the most outstanding feature of Sierra Leone's cultural life is its dancing. The Sierra Leone Dance Troupe is internationally known. There are elements of symbolism in most of their dances—drums, wooden xylophones and various stringed instruments provide the musical background.

6

Down With Colonial Rule

When independence came throughout Africa, it all happened in a histori-cally short period of time. Some countries became republics almost simultaneously. By the early 1960s most former European colonies had been given the opportunity to decide for themselves who would lead them toward the twenty-first century. Invariably, they chose independence.

Independence in French West Africa

Shortly after World War II, France's eight West African territories were proclaimed members of the French Union. The Africans living there were made French citizens. It was another ten years, however, before the natives were allowed to vote. By then, the French government at home was in transition and French holdings in West Africa were on the brink of falling apart. In 1958 France granted the colonies self-governing status as countries within the new French Community— although Paris insisted on keeping several important powers, including control over foreign, military, and economic affairs.

The people of French Guinea rejected the plan, turning away from the French Community and voting for full independence in September 1958. This vote plunged Guinea into an immediate crisis, because Paris abruptly pulled its colonial administration—along with vital goods and equipment—out of the feisty former colony. Before it could steady itself as an independent nation, Guinea was on the verge of bankruptcy.

For the moment, the other territories chose to remain part of the French Community. Within months, though, they began forging their own independent plans. Senegal and French Sudan briefly merged to become the Federation of Mali. In 1960 they separated again; the former French Sudan became the Republic of Mali. By the end of that year, Dahomey, Haute-Volta (Upper Volta), the Ivory Coast, Mauritania, and Niger also had become independent republics. They soon joined the United Nations.

The new republics' early leaders were men who had been at the forefront of political activities in the post–World War II era. For example, the ten blacks elected to the French National Assembly in 1946 included Léopold-Sédar Senghor, who became Senegal's first president in 1960, and Félix Houphouët-Boigny, a pro-French native who led Côte d'Ivoire during its first three decades of local rule. Throughout former French West Africa, the new nations have maintained close economic ties with France.

INDEPENDENCE IN THE BRITISH WEST AFRICAN COLONIES

As we saw earlier, native blacks of the Gold Coast in the early 1950s were given control over their colony's governing assembly. Kwame Nkrumah, the colony's leader in its drive for independence, diplomatically made further gains for his people

Group of Dancers, Sierra Leone, c. 1890 (T. J. Alldridge).

during the next several years. In March 1957 the long-time colony was made a sovereign country—though it remained within the British Commonwealth. Nkrumah was its prime minister. In 1960 it became the totally independent Republic of Ghana. At the time, many Africans saw Nkrumah as the potential leader of a continent-wide, independent socialist state.

Other British colonies, inspired by the political success of Nkrumah in the Gold Coast, by that time were on the verge of independence as well. British Prime Minister Harold McMillan, touring Africa in early 1960, commented on the "wind of change" that was fanning the whole continent. He sensed a very strong "African national consciousness" among native peoples. But black leaders who clamored for self-rule in these countries perhaps failed to realize how their situations differed from that of Nkrumah and his followers in the Gold Coast. For one thing, their colonies did not enjoy the same level of prosperity that blessed the Gold Coast during the 1950s thanks to high world prices for cocoa. And there were other difficulties.

In Nigeria, as we noted earlier, serious conflicts had existed for centuries between the Muslim-led people in the north and the black African-dominated population of the south. In 1957 Great Britain divided Nigeria into three geographic regions, each with a limited degree of self-government. Until that time, political leaders in the north would not commit to a push for national independence because they feared southern leaders would take control of the new nation. After the division, however, they played a wily political move: they negotiated a coalition with the National Convention of Nigerian Citizens, the dominant political faction in the east, and called for independence. With this alliance, the northerners believed they could establish themselves firmly in a nationwide government.

Independence came to Nigeria in October 1960 but did nothing to resolve regional animosity. Within a decade, Nigeria was embroiled in a catastrophic civil war.

Sierra Leone became independent in April 1961. Here the most worrisome internal division was between the Freetown citizens—Creoles, descendants of the freed slaves who had settled there the century before—and the native tribes elsewhere. By and large, the Creoles were better educated and more prosperous. These discrepancies would result in strife for independent Sierra Leone.

The Gambia, in part because of its tiny size, was the last British West African colony to achieve independence. It declared its autonomy in February 1965 and became a republic in 1970. From 1982 to 1989, The Gambia and Senegal formed a confederation called Senegambia, combining their military forces and cooperating in economic policies. Irreconcilable disputes soon ended the collaborative experiment.

Bambara Hunters, Sierra Leone c. 1890 (T. J. Alldridge).
Alldridge photographed these three Bambara hunters about 150 miles inland. Hunting methods there probably had not changed in centuries. The Bambara are a linguistic group of the upper Niger region who have intermingled with other tribes. Within each of their small villages is a dominant family which provides a chief, or fama, *who has virtually absolute power.*

Ousting the Portuguese and Spanish

Years after France and England had turned control of their former West African colonies over to the natives, Portugal clung to its small holdings, Portuguese Guinea (Guinea-Bissau) and Cape Verde. Although greatly diminished as an international power since its early centuries of maritime importance, Portugal was the first European country to subdue parts of Africa, and one of the very last to leave.

Impatient nationalists, inspired by the political victories of their neighboring countries, went to war against the colonial administration in Portuguese Guinea in 1962. Over a period of twelve years, rebel guerrillas drove the Portuguese from most regions of the country.

General Antonio de Spinola, who commanded the Portuguese military in West Africa during the early 1970s, himself favored independence for the colony. His forces steadily were losing ground to nationalist rebels, and Spinola realized it could not be retaken. In fact, by 1973 the people of the liberated parts of the territory had elected their own government assembly and declared the independent state of Guinea-Bissau.

Spinola saw that the prolonged war in Africa was devastating Portugal's home economy, and in 1974 he led the so-called Armed Forces Movement in a military coup that overthrew Portugal's longstanding fascist dictatorship at home. Under the new government, Portugal quickly acknowledged Guinea-Bissau's independence. Self-rule soon followed in other Portuguese colonies in Africa, including Cape Verde in 1975.

While Portugal waged its losing campaign to retain Guinea-Bissau, Spain fidgeted over what to do with Spanish Sahara (now Western Sahara). Spain was loath to give up the territory because of a particular natural resource: phosphate. Meanwhile, the neighboring countries of Morocco, Mauritania, and Algeria wanted to claim all or portions of the colony. In 1976 Spain finally pulled out of the territory and Moroccan and Mauritanian forces moved in, dividing Western Sahara between them. A bizarre power struggle ensued, as we'll see in the next chapter.

ON THEIR OWN

As the colonial administrators withdrew, westerners hoped the newly independent African countries would establish healthy democracies and maintain friendly commercial ties with free world countries. They were appalled by news accounts that soon emerged from all across the continent: reports of military takeovers and civil wars, gruesome details of human suffering and death.

Observers hardly should have been surprised, however. Some colonial officials had warned for years that the Africans were not prepared to govern themselves. In at least one sense, they were correct. It was virtually impossible for most of the new countries to establish internal unity. The colonial regimes had left them with geographic boundaries that suited the Europeans' purposes but made no sense to the tribal groups. The leaders of a typical republic in the new Africa now had to try to satisfy the demands of many political parties, most of them eager for power. Some of the factions immediately pressed for secession into smaller countries. In a way, a brand new "scramble for Africa" was underway from within.

Internal divisions hampered economic development—which would be difficult enough even under peaceful conditions. The Europeans had been interested only in taking from Africa the continent's natural resources, as easily and cheaply as possible; they had made no effort to prepare the natives for self-rule. After independence, worsening economies led to deep discontent among the people. The stage was set for a quarter-century of horrible poverty, fighting, and failed governments.

Bambara Dwarf, Sierra Leone, c. 1890 (T. J. Alldridge). *The Bambara people, a branch of the Niger-Congo language group, had a remarkable system of metaphysics and cosmology that included animalistic cults and myths. The Bambara were noted for their* segoni-kun, *or stylized masks. These masks were worn by dancers at special cultivation and harvest rites. This Bambara dwarf was believed to possess magical powers.*

7

WEST AFRICA SINCE INDEPENDENCE

Within a period of fifteen years, all of West Africa became self-governing except Western Sahara, where Moroccans still vied against native nationalists to take over the country. The result of West African independence was by no means instant happiness.

Political unrest in the newly independent countries was what the world saw through news reports during the late 1900s. In some countries, a military faction would seize control of the government, only to be overthrown by another faction within months. A seemingly hopeless assortment of problems plagued each new government: poor national economies, tribal conflicts, government corruption. Problems were particularly glaring in sub-Saharan countries like Niger and Mali that could produce comparatively few exportable crops and were ravaged by droughts. Throughout the "bulge," military coups were practically as common as popular elections.

As American politicians know, the economy usually has more impact on election results than any other campaign issue. It influences almost every measurable gauge of

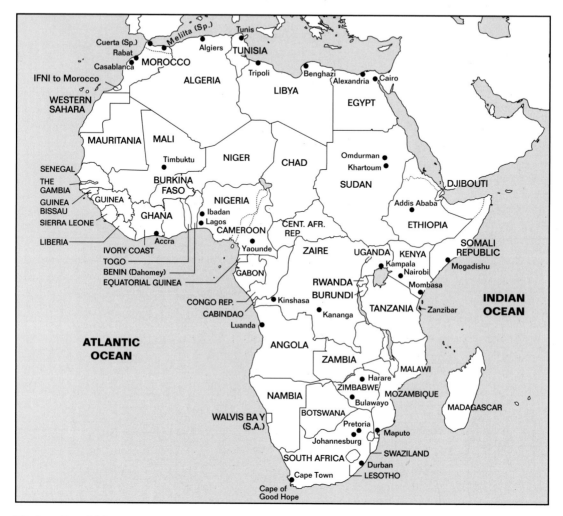

Modern Day Africa

a country's health, from personal and family prosperity to the quality of education to public confidence—even to national security. In West Africa, since independence, the economy has been generally dismal. Some new nations have such scarce natural resources and poorly developed agricultural programs that their populations remain below the poverty level. Others face complicated obstacles in plying their exports in the world market. All too often, African nations have found themselves importing more than they can export, borrowing from foreign countries with no foreseeable means of repaying, and—although independent—depending on foreign assistance. Many African nations now are having trouble just paying the interest on their overseas debt.

Government corruption and industrial mismanagement have worsened the affairs of many republics. Distrust and strife among religious factions have made West Africa's modernization efforts even more difficult. Essentially, these divisions existed before the European colonists arrived, and rather than uniting the peoples who followed different faiths, the colonial system fed their animosity. For example, Muslims in some areas accused white bureaucrats of favoring Christian blacks when hiring native clerks.

Let's look at each West African Republic in turn.

Benin

Benin's people descend from many different kingdoms and tribes. Some of their ancestors were based in areas that now are part of other West African nations. Examples are the Ewe language group that originated in Tado (in present-day Togo) and the Bariba group that belonged to a confederacy spanning parts of Nigeria. When the Europeans began trading in the lower coast of the "bulge" during the 1500s, Benin became a thriving slave outlet.

About two thirds of the country's people still hold to ancient religions. Most others are divided evenly between Christians and Muslims. French, as in most other former French West Africa colonies, is the main language of the educated class. Natives fish along the sandbar-lined coast and farm vegetables and fruits in the tropical interior. Porto-Novo is the seaport capital.

Palm oil, used in soap making, is Benin's main export. The republic also produces significant quantities of coffee and cotton.

Called Dahomey until 1967, Benin, like other French territories, became a self-ruling republic of the new French Community in the late 1950s. It achieved full independence in August 1960 . . . and entered an era of internal political divisions and military coups, aggravated by a failing economy. By 1972

Benin had been the scene of no fewer than six military take-overs of the government.

A sense of stability was effected after an officer named Mathieu Kérékou rose to power in 1972. For fifteen years, Kérékou embraced a fundamental communistic doctrine—then veered toward democratic ideals. After almost two decades of leadership, he was defeated in the country's 1991 presidential elections by Nicéphore Soglo. Five years later, Kérékou won reelection over Soglo, inheriting a nation with a chronically ill economy, groping for ways toward progress as a member of the world community. At this writing, the country was preparing for its 2001 presidential election.

BURKINA FASO

After a prelude of explorations and military expeditions by Germans and French, France brought under its "protection" various pieces of territory north of the Gold Coast during the 1890s. In 1919 France organized them into a colony named Haute-Volta (Upper Volta). This became a partly self-governing country within the French Union in 1947, became a republic within the French Community in 1958, and achieved complete independence in August 1960.

The new nation drafted a constitution calling for an elective form of government. Military leaders, however, often have imposed authoritarian regimes—a sometimes peaceful, some-times violent procedure common in independent Africa. Gen-eral Sangoulé Lamizana took control in 1966 and remained in power until 1980. Military coups succeeded in that year and again in 1982. Captain Thomas Sankara became head of state and in 1984 gave the country a hopeful new name: Burkina Faso, "Land of Incorruptible People." Sankara demanded that government officials be held up to public scrutiny. He took sig-nificant steps to improve health and living conditions and streamline the government. Unfortunately, in 1987, he was slain in a bloody coup led by three army officers with whom he had shared power. One of the three, Captain Blaise Compaoré, became leader of the so-called Popular Front and the country's head of state. He continued to hold control through the 1990s.

Mande Men, Sierra Leone, c. 1890 (T. J. Alldridge). *These Mande men are playing the traditional* sangboi, *or tomtom. The Mande are an agricultural people. Their principal crops are corn, sorghum, and rice. Cattle are raised—but are important mainly for prestige and bride-price payment.*

Situated near the lower reaches of the Sahara, Burkina Faso strongly feels the North African Muslim influence. About half its people are Muslims, 40 percent followers of native beliefs, and a small percentage Christians. It has only river ports, being hundreds of miles from the Gulf of Guinea. The capital is Ouagadougou. French is the official language, but most rural people speak in tribal tongues, mainly of the Sudanic language group.

Most of the terrain is savanna. Millet, sorghum, and other crops are grown, and several notable minerals are extracted. Burkina Faso relies heavily on foreign assistance, though. Thousands of rural people each year flock southward to relocate in Ghana and Côte d'Ivoire.

CAPE VERDE

If you are interested in meteorology—weather watching—you probably know that many Atlantic hurricanes originate off the West African coast. In this storm-breeding nest lie the Cape Verde Islands, officially known as the Republic of Cape Verde. The island republic is almost 400 miles west of Senegal.

Portugal controlled the islands from around 1460 until it granted independence in 1975. The islands were uninhabited when the Portuguese arrived. Colonists soon came from Portugal, and black slaves were transported out from West Africa. Today most island residents are Creoles of mixed European and African descent. Portuguese is the primary language, and the principal island religion is based on Roman Catholicism and native beliefs.

Fifteen volcanic islands (one still active) make up Cape Verde. Some are rugged and barely inhabitable, with steep-cliffed coastlines. Others have flat plains and valleys. The capital, Praia, is on the island of São Tiago.

Naturally, much of the livelihood in Cape Verde is taken from the sea. Fish and salt are among the republic's leading resources, as well as bananas and coffee. Curiously, despite its tropical oceanic location, the islands have been plagued by droughts, requiring substantial foreign aid and resulting in the deaths of some 200,000 people during the past century.

Lightly populated (about half a million people), the islands fare better than most African countries. The literacy rate is almost 50 percent (comparatively high), and the infant mortality rate is between 5 and 6 percent (the lowest among West African republics). Those kinds of statistics generally are much worse on the mainland.

Political stress also has been relatively low. Antonio Mascarenhas Monteiro was elected president in 1991 and reelected in 1996. Several officials had announced their candidacies for president in the 2001 election as this book was being written.

Perhaps the most interesting statistic about Cape Verde is that more than half its people are children and teenagers! As they reach adulthood, most islanders go to Europe and South America to find work and establish themselves.

Town Drums in Susu Village, Sierra Leone, c. 1890 (T. J. Alldridge). *The Susu people live in the southern coastal regions of Guinea and the northwestern parts of Sierra Leone. In Sierra Leone, Susu villages are grouped around a chief. Several villages form a chiefdom and number 3,000–6,000 persons. This photograph is of a village near Falaba, the Susu capital. The town drums are in the center of the village's main open space.*

CÔTE D'IVOIRE

Elephants abounded here when the Europeans arrived, giving the country its name: the Ivory Coast. Today, the elephant population is alarmingly reduced, but the country remains one of beauty. The land rises from the coast through jungles, savannas, and, in the northwest, mountains.

Farming is Côte d'Ivoire's primary occupation. The country is a world leader in exporting coffee and cocoa. It also is noted for its timber industry, exporting great quantities of African woods.

Interestingly, Côte d'Ivoire has two "capitals." Yamoussoukro was made the official capital in 1983, but Abidjan, Côte d'Ivoire's former capital and main port, still houses many government offices. Abidjan is typical of modern African seaport cities. Skyscrapers and elegant hotels and homes stand not far from saddening slums. Spread along a peaceful lagoon, Abidjan is picturesque when viewed from the lush green shore across the water. But it is also a working city—the largest oceanic container port in West Africa.

Though officially French-speaking, Côte d'Ivoire is diverse in tribal languages. About a fourth of its people have kept their ancient religions, which teach that spirits—some friendly, some evil—reside in people, animals, and inert objects like stones and trees. Islam is strong in the capital and in the north of the country. Christianity also is prominent.

With its broad mix of tongues, cultures, and traditional customs, Côte d'Ivoire is world-renowned for its fascinating variety of native dancing, music, wood carvings, and other arts. However, these same tribal differences have made it hard for "Ivorians" to unite themselves.

Félix Houphouët-Boigny was elected president when Côte d'Ivoire became independent in 1960 and served three decades. Like many other African leaders during the early decades of independence, Houphouët-Boigny governed as a political strongman, with little tolerance for opposing parties. Yet, he is credited with instilling a much needed sense of unity across the land.

Henri Konan Bédié became head of state in 1993. A military coup rocked the country in December 1999, followed the next year by the election of Laurent Gagbo as president. Gagbo was reforming the government in January 2001 as ethnic divisions paralyzed the country's political scene.

THE GAMBIA

Encouragingly, some African nations during the 1990s moved toward truly democratic forms of government—at least in theory. In The Gambia, military strongman Yahya Jammeh

Weaving Loom in Susu Village, Sierra Leone, c. 1890 (T. J. Alldridge). *This weaving loom was located in a Susu village at Massaia, near Falaba. The principal industry throughout this entire area was the weaving of cotton into cloth. The texture of the cloth was coarse and the colors, all made from vegetable dyes, retained their brightness after repeated washings. The cloth was made on a primitive wooden loom in long strips only a few inches in width.*

There are at least eighteen ethnic groups in Sierra Leone. All have common cultural features such as secret societies, chieftains, and farming methods. The social structures are also similar—a hierarchical ordering from royalty and noble lineages to commoners, artisan castes, and former slaves. Every Susu belongs to a patrilineal clan that can be identified by name. Most claim to be Muslims. Weavers, shoemakers, jewelers, musicians, smiths, and carpenters formerly constituted separate castes and are said to be descended from slaves.

led a 1994 coup that deposed long-time president Dawda Jawara. Jammeh led an oppressive government, putting down political opposition. After the people voted for a new constitution in 1996, however, Jammeh left the army, ran for president, and was duly elected. Thus, a former dictator became a bona fide, representative head of state—although Jammeh continued to exert stern control over the country.

A splinter of land, just fifteen to thirty miles wide and driven several hundred miles from the western coast into the "bulge," The Gambia spans the banks of the River Gambia. It is enveloped all around by Senegal—a radical example of the weird way West Africa was partitioned through European power struggles and compromises.

The lower river area is swampland, rising to the *banto faros* flatlands in the middle course and to highlands farther inland. Most of the farming people live upstream, away from swamps with their flood hazards. Villagers grow peanuts as a cash crop and live on cassava and yams (root crops) and other subsistence items. A fledgling fishing industry works the river and coast. The country's capital is the port city of Banjul.

Relying so heavily on peanut production, The Gambia's overall economy is at the mercy of droughts. Living conditions here are among the worst in West Africa, with an infant mortality rate of around 17 percent and an average life expectancy only in the low 40s.

Since gaining its independence from Great Britain, The Gambia has retained English as its official language. The vast majority of Gambians are Muslims.

GHANA

The British-controlled Gold Coast got its name from early coastal trade. Europeans exchanged cloth, tools, liquor, guns, and trinkets for gold brought by natives from the interior. As the modern Republic of Guinea, the old colony is noted for a much less sinister type of "gold": cocoa, the raw ingredient of chocolate. During the colonial era, this became the world's leading source of cocoa. As a result, the Gold Coast was Great Britain's most successful African colony economically. Its per capita revenue became the highest in West Africa, and it was able to establish a comparatively good system of transportation. Farming and mining activities thrived.

Group of Musicians in Susu Village, Sierra Leone, c. 1890 (T. J. Alldridge). *This photograph of a group of Susu musicians playing xylophones was taken in Falaba, the Susu capital. Falaba is located in the extreme northwest of Sierra Leone, near the Guinea border. Alexander Laing (1793–1826), the Scottish explorer and the first known European to have reached the ancient West African city of Tombouctou [Timbuktu], visited the Susu people and Falaba in 1822–1823. His published journals (1825) are the earliest European descriptions of the interior peoples of Sierra Leone.*

After World War II, Kwame Nkrumah became the colony's leading native political leader. The Gold Coast obtained a large measure of self-government in the early 1950s, with Nkrumah at the head of a primarily native administration. In 1957 Nkrumah's Convention People's Party led the emergence of Ghana, as the colony was renamed, into the United Nations as an independent member of the British Commonwealth. It became a republic in 1960.

Although Nkrumah for a while was regarded as a possible leader of a pan-African alliance, his popular stature steadily diminished when Ghana's economy failed and its government slipped into corruption. He was deposed in a 1966 coup. There followed a seesaw pattern of military and civilian regimes, with no leader holding power for more than a few years until Jerry Rawlings, a Ghanian air force officer, seized control in 1981 and established a governing body called the Provisional National Defense Council. Rawlings banned political parties in the country. Elected president in 1992 and again in 1996, he was ousted by voters in January 2001, when John Agyekum Kufour became president.

Ghana's stature in the world community received a notable boost in 1997 when one of its natives, Kofi Annan, became secretary-general of the United Nations.

English remains the official language of Ghana. Its people are divided spiritually between native, Muslim, and Christian faiths.

GUINEA

Guinea is a beautiful, diverse country that reaches meanderingly from a lush, tropical Atlantic coast to pasturelands and mountains well inside the continent's "bulge." On its northeastern border with Mali it touches the lower edge of the arid Saharan expanse.

Sékou Touré was Guinea's leader for independence. In the 1950s he and his followers began demanding racial equality, a native voice in government, and educational and employment improvements for blacks. Touré once stated that native Guineans preferred "poverty in liberty to riches in slavery." In 1958 the people voted to make Guinea the first French West African country fully independent of France, and Touré was elected president. He served until his death in 1984, keeping tight check over opposition political parties; some of his opponents were jailed, tortured, even killed.

The military took control of the government after Touré's death. Free elections began in 1993, and General Lansana

Two Musicians in Sulima, Sierra Leone, c. 1890 (T. J. Alldridge). *Alldridge photographed these musicians in Sulima, a coastal town on the Liberian border. The Sulima area was rich in palm oil and, as Alldridge noted, "the quantity exported is nothing to the enormous mass that is untouched, simply from want of the means of transport." These men are xylophone players. The xylophone is one of the principal instruments of African music, being found in many forms. It is known in Latin America as the marimba and was probably taken there by African slaves.*

Conté became president. His tenure, which continued into 2001, has been marked by charges of election irregularities and a foiled military mutiny.

French is the country's official language, although only a small fraction of its people speak the colonial language. Many citizens descend from time-honored West African kingdoms like the Malinké and Fulani. Almost three fourths of the people follow Islam; others are Christians or believers in ancient African religious teachings.

Aluminum (bauxite) and iron ore are Guinea's main natural resources. Its people mine a significant quantity of diamonds and gold. The great majority of Guineans, however, are either subsistence farmers or growers of marketable cash crops. Cassava, rice, corn, bananas, and coffee are among the country's other export foods. A notable fishing industry works the coastal waters.

GUINEA-BISSAU

Portugal's dominion over its long-time colony was basically peaceful between World War I and the beginning of Africa's succession of independent nations in the 1950s and 1960s. Seeing their neighbors win self-rule, activists in Portuguese Guinea began calling for a break from Portugal.

A nationalist group, the African Party for the Independence of Guinea and Cape Verde, began organizing poor farmers into guerilla units, striking Portuguese government offices and armed forces installations in the early 1960s. For more than a decade, led by Amílcar Cabral, the rebels persisted, gradually taking over most of the colony's interior. Cabral was assassinated in 1973, but the following year, Portugal underwent a government coup at home. The new Lisbon regime granted independence to its former West African holding, which the rebel government already had renamed Guinea-Bissau. Luis Cabral, half-brother of the martyred freedom fighter, became the new republic's first president.

Military officers in 1980 toppled the government and did away with the elected national assembly. Brigadier General Joao Bernardo Vieira assumed power. By the mid-1990s, an elective government had been restored. Peace here, as in many African countries, has been elusive, though. Military officers revolted in 1998. The government quelled the action with the help of troops sent from neighboring Senegal. President Kumba Yala in early 2001 was having to reorganize his cabinet because of political dissensions.

Portuguese is Guinea-Bissau's official language. About two thirds of the people practice native religions; most others are Muslims. Much of the country is coastal swampland. Nuts, fruits, and vegetables are grown, and mines produce bauxite and phosphates. Bissau is the capital and primary port city.

"Devil Dance" in Sulima, Sierra Leone, c. 1890 (T. J. Alldridge).
This is a rare photograph of "the Nefari Devil Dance" performed in Sulima, a coastal town in the southern part of Sierra Leone. The male performer is accompanied by a musician who provides the rhythmic beat. Local people believed that evil spirits lived under rocks, on isolated mountain tops, etc., and that this dance would repel them.

Health conditions are poor compared to some of the other West African countries, but the literacy rate—around 55 percent—is relatively high.

LIBERIA

We've devoted a full chapter to Liberia (pages 60–69), which stands uniquely as the only African nation to escape European colonization.

MALI

A large, land-locked nation, the Republic of Mali was part of France's sprawling desert territory during colonization. In the southern part of the country, where the Niger makes its great arc, Mali features grasslands supporting varied wildlife, including elephants and other large beasts for which Africa is famous. North of the ancient city of Timbuktu, Mali opens into the seemingly endless, barren Sahara Desert. In colonial days, the region was called French Sudan.

When France underwent its governmental transition in 1958, what is now Mali became the Sudanese Republic (not to be confused with the country of Sudan, far to the east) in the new French Community. The next year, it joined Senegal as part of a federation that native leaders hoped would attract neighboring territories. The union quickly failed, and Senegal and Mali in 1960 became separate republics. Modibo Keita, a Marxist politician, became Mali's first president and developed close ties with the USSR and its satellites.

Dissatisfaction with Keita's rule inspired a military coup in 1968. Lieutenant Moussa Traoré took power and, during the 1970s when a civilian government was reestablished, was elected president. He improved diplomatic relations with France and the United States, seeking foreign assistance for Mali, while continuing to support communist bloc countries. Traoré was ousted in 1991, and Alpha Oumar Konare became president the following year. Konare was reelected in 1997 amid complaints of election irregularities; his term extends until 2002.

Not over-blessed with natural resources, Mali has been hurt by droughts since independence. The World Food Programme approved a multimillion-dollar famine relief package for Mali as recently as January 2001. The nation's people grow millet, rice, and other crops, and mine gold and phosphates. Many are nomadic herders. River fishing provides livelihoods in the lower regions of the country.

Bamako, near the headwaters of the River Niger, is Mali's capital. Some 90 percent of its people are Muslim. French is the official language.

Slave Market in Mongeri, Sierra Leone, c. 1890 (T. J. Alldridge). *This photograph was taken in the slave market of Mongeri, a town in the central part of Sierra Leone. During the American Revolution (1775–1783), Great Britain promised freedom to those slaves who fled from their rebel masters and joined the British military. (At the start of the American Revolution, slavery was legal in twelve of the thirteen colonies, the exception being Massachusetts.) Although Great Britain did create a special fighting corps, called the Black Pioneers, most blacks in the British army were used for menial work.*

At the end of the American Revolution, Great Britain offered all colonists who had supported them, including the now freed blacks, resettlement in Nova Scotia. However, Thomas Peters, a former sergeant in the Black Pioneers, instead led about 1,200 black Loyalists in fifteen ships to Sierra Leone. Financed by London philanthropists, this group, and their descendants, are known as "the Nova Scotians." They gave the name "Freetown" to the port city they built.

From 1807, when Great Britain outlawed the slave trade, to 1864 more than 50,000 "recaptive" slaves were brought into Freetown by British naval ships. Drawn from all over western Africa, this heterogeneous people lacked a common language and culture. But the Freetown government had a deliberate policy of turning these people into productive citizens, and for the most part, they succeeded. The "recaptives" and their descendants are known as Creoles or Krios.

The Freetown government was unable to extend its antislavery policies throughout the rest of Sierra Leone until about 1900. Between 1888 and 1900, Great Britain moved to control the Sierra Leone interior, and wherever the British exercised authority, slavery and the slave trade finally ended.

MAURITANIA

As its name suggests, the Islamic Republic of Mauritania long has been almost wholly dominated by Moorish people of the Islamic religion, both in the life of its citizens and in the focus of its government. It is generally a flat, dry country marked by plateaus and sand dunes. Unlike most other West African countries along the southern Sahara, though, Mauritania has the advantage of more than 400 miles of Atlantic coastline. Fishing is profitable at Lévier Bay; the fish are packed and processed at the port city of Nouadhibou. Nouakchott, Mauritania's other major seaport to the south, is the national capital.

Also distinct from most former French West African colonies, Mauritania has not kept French as its official language; Arabic and native black languages dominate. Much buying and selling among the people still is done by the age-old barter system, wherein they trade goods, not cash. Pack animals commonly are used for transport and travel. Only one main road, which enters neighboring Algeria in the northeast, can be traversed year-round.

As in neighboring Mali and other desert countries, many Mauritanians are nomads who herd livestock. Near the River Senegal and Mauritania's southern border with Mali, lions, elephants, antelope, and other large animals can be seen. Livestock grazing and farming is possible here. In the north, however, most life is confined to desert oases where water can be found.

Iron deposits attracted foreign companies in the early years of Mauritania's independence, but the country's iron resources have dwindled. Mauritanians also mine copper.

Since Mauritania's independence in 1960, civilian governments twice have been overturned by the military. Political opposition parties, banned for years, were legalized in 1991, and President Maouya Ould Sid'Ahmed Taya took office in 1992. Appallingly, an estimated 90,000 people in Mauritania are kept in virtual slavery, and thousands of citizens have been deported. Health care is generally outdated, and some two thirds of Mauritanians are illiterate.

Buduma Canoe on Lake Chad, c. 1912–1917 (Jean Tilho). *Lake Chad is the largest lake in western Africa, about 7,000 square miles. (The Great Salt Lake in Utah is approximately 2,400 square miles.) It is the remnant of a much larger, very deep, ancient sea that drained into the Atlantic Ocean. At the conjunction of the nations of Chad, Cameroon, Nigeria, and Niger, this inhospitable desert area of Africa was among the last to be explored by Europeans.*

Exploring the Lake Chad region became a passion for Colonel Jean Tilho (1875–1956) of the French Colonial Military. Tilho ranks as one of the early twentieth century's most dashing adventurers. He accomplished daring military exploits against Saharan desert tribes who resisted French domination and made his own maps of many areas. He wrote,

> *From my early youth I had felt myself irresistibly drawn toward Africa, and I was filled with a desire to share in the discoveries of great explorers, whose intrepid expeditions had revealed to the civilized world some part of the mysterious and immense dark continent . . . I would ponder over the map of Africa, and amid great blank spaces in the centre of the continent, appeared but a few geographical features—one of which, Lake Chad, coloured in blue, possessed a special fascination for me.*

During 1912–1917 Tilho obsessively devoted himself to his hypothesis that millenniums ago, Lake Chad had been linked to the Nile 1,200 miles to the west and that on the banks of that ancient river connection, through the now deserts of central Africa, had once existed one of the most brilliant and ancient civilizations of the world. His dispatches from the deserts of Libya, Sudan, and Chad were avidly followed by his devoted readers, and a new radio link from the antenna atop the Eiffel Tower further contributed to the excitement generated by his exploits. T. E. Lawrence (Lawrence of Arabia), another archaeological scholar and military strategist, avidly followed Tilho's adventures. In 1918 The Royal Geographical Society awarded Colonel Tilho the Royal Medal, its highest honor.

NIGER

Niger is largely a Saharan—but mountainous—country. Along the southern border with Nigeria, however, grasslands support rich wildlife. Niger is one of the new African nations where Muslim influences of the north meet the black traditions of the sub-Sahara.

Because of its distance from both the Gulf of Guinea and the Mediterranean Sea, the land that is modern Niger was among the last African territories to be explored substantially by Europeans. Not until the late 1700s did the first investigators spend much time so far inland, and most of the ensuing probes—and power plays—were along the River Niger. France claimed the region during the late-nineteenth-century "scramble for Africa," but a military expedition it sent into the colony in 1899 was stubbornly resisted. Only after World War I did France install a bona fide colonial administration.

Like other French West African colonies, Niger was given independence in a series of policy changes from Paris beginning after World War II. In 1958 its people voted to remain part of the French Community. Two years later, Niger became a fully independent republic. Then Hamani Diori ruled the country as a dictator, from 1960 to 1974, when the military overthrew him. In 1993 Niger held free elections, and Mahamane Ousmane was chosen president. The military took control again three years later. General Ibrahim Bare Mainassara assumed the presidency and later was elected, though in controversial balloting. He was assassinated in April 1999. Mamadou Tandja subsequently was elected president.

Most people in Niger farm or herd livestock. As in other sub-Saharan countries, Niger farmers have to contend with a unique natural problem: the gradual encroachment of the awesome Sahara Desert into fringe lands that once could sustain cattle and subsistence farming. Perpetual drought has caused ongoing strife in modern times.

Oddly enough, the mighty river from which Niger takes its name slices through only the far western arm of the country. Niamey, a major river port, is Niger's capital. French is the official language.

Natives Listening to a Gramophone, Chad, c. 1907–1909 (Jean Tilho). *In 1899 Chad was ceded to France under an Anglo-French agreement. However, pacification of the various peoples proved to be almost impossible, as enmities between the north and the south could not be resolved. Chad became part of French Equatorial Africa in 1920.*

Previous to his 1912–1917 explorations, Captain Jean Tilho had been assigned to survey the conflicting boundary claims in west-central Africa of France, Great Britain, and Germany (1907–1909). Tilho's final report was supplemented by his personal observations about ethnography and natural science. It is estimated that he traveled some 25,000 miles during these two years—a contemporary wrote the Tilho's study "appeals to the imagination [because of] the vast and strange country it concerns."

This is a photograph taken in southern Chad of natives listening to a gramophone. A local emir is seated on a carpet in the center. Tilho's staff carried this gramophone on their extensive mapping expedition to both awe and to placate the local people.

Niger since independence has managed to become a world player in the production of peanuts and other crops, and in the mining of such materials as uranium. Overall, however, its resources are underdeveloped, and its standard of living is among the worst in the world.

Nigeria

For a hundred yards or more, rows upon rows of wooden barrels containing palm oil lined the banks of Niger delta ports during the colonial era. They awaited ocean shipment to England, where palm oil provided the basis for soap, margarine, and other products.

Nigeria—the most heavily populated nation in Africa—was and remains a country rich in natural enticements to foreign importers. The River Niger and colonial railway and road systems bring cocoa, palm oil, corn, yams, and other food products to dockyards for foreign shipment. The country also abounds in crude oil and other natural resources. Coastal and river fishing long has been a thriving occupation for natives in marine areas.

Among the African nations, Nigeria is especially rich in tribal, cultural, and religious diversity. Most of the continent's ancient races can be found here, from the Hausa and Fulani people in the north to the Yoruba in the southwest and the Igbo in the southeast. Christianity spread widely through the Niger delta in the south before and during the colonial era. Many of Nigeria's 250 ethnic groups still adhere to primitive religious practices. Today the republic's constitution guarantees religious freedom, but Muslim fundamentalists in recent decades have waged anti-Christian persecution in parts of the country.

The prospect of unifying Nigeria has baffled leaders since early colonial days. In 1967 the country erupted into civil war when the Igbo people of the east declared their independence as the new country of Biafra. Forces from other parts of Nigeria ended the attempt and reunited the republic after three years of the bloodiest, costliest struggle in modern Africa.

Since then, Nigeria has seen a succession of armed coups and violence so appalling that in 1995 international sanctions were imposed against the regime of General Sani Abacha. Political dissenters have been imprisoned, sometimes executed. Abacha died in 1998 and was succeeded by General Abdulsalam Abubakar. In 1999 the military negotiated a transfer of power with the leaders of Nigeria's three main political parties. Olusegun Obasanjo was elected president.

Abuja in 1991 was made the national capital, replacing the port of Lagos. Interestingly, Abuja was developed during the 1980s for the specific purpose of becoming the capital, being located near the geographic center of the republic.

Buduma Village, c. 1912–1917 (Jean Tilho). *The Lake Chad region contains evidence of very early human life. Jean Tilho believed that there was a constant human development here which reached its zenith with a great civilization concurrent with the pharaonic dynasties of Egypt. During the medieval period (ninth through sixteenth centuries), Lake Chad was an important area where powerful kingdoms united diverse populations. However, certain groups resisted this integration. The Buduma were such a people.*

This photograph is of a Buduma village located on an island in Lake Chad. The Buduma, who also are found in Chad, Cameroon, and Nigeria, established themselves on these inaccessible islands and along the marshy northern shore of Lake Chad. These sedentary people live in huts that vary from those made of straw to those made of hardened mud.

SENEGAL

European explorers and traders had an early impact on Senegal, where they found brown-skinned, thick-lipped, flat-nosed peoples descended from ancient tribes: Wolof, Fulani, Malinké, and others. Through intermarriage with the Berbers to the north, Senegalese gradually developed into a taller, more fine-featured group, fondly regarded for their tradition of hospitality. Three fourths of them are Muslims, the rest followers of traditional native religions and, along the coast, Christianity.

Senegal's capital is Dakar, the largest seaport in West Africa. After its establishment in 1857, Dakar became a leading commercial center linking European and interior traders.

French is Senegal's national language, though some tribes retain their native tongues. About 75 percent of the citizens farm or have agriculture-related jobs, and most people live in small rural villages. Peanuts, millet, and sorghum are among the republic's staple crops, but many villagers are subsistence farmers. Phosphate, used to make fertilizer, detergents, and other chemicals, is the most important trade resource. Senegal also has a significant fishing industry, especially on the Atlantic coast.

Although primarily agricultural, Senegal is the most industrialized of the former French West African colonies. Food processing, oil refining, and chemical manufacturing are leading industries.

A relatively flat land, Senegal is situated in the region where dry Saharan air collides with moisture from the Atlantic Ocean and thus has a heavy average rainfall. Although the human population has claimed much of the habitat in the vicinity of the coast, a rich variety of wild animals still roam the inland expanses.

Independent since 1960, Senegal adopted its first constitution in 1963. This nation is a democracy, with an elected president, a National Assembly, and ten "states" overseen by governors. Léopold-Sédar Senghor was Senegal's president until 1981, when he was succeeded by Abdou Diouf. Senghor led Senegal with an iron grip, suppressing political opposition parties. Abdoulaye Wade became president in 2000.

Senegal continues to maintain close ties with France, which has provided much needed financial aid. Since the country's economy depends heavily on the peanut crop, its national health is at the mercy of the weather on one hand and international agricultural markets on the other.

SIERRA LEONE

Like Liberia, Sierra Leone is known as a land of freed slaves. But whereas Liberia maintained independence during the colonial period, Sierra Leone was an English colony. Freetown, the republic's appropriately named capital, became a

Rock Drawings, Borkou, Chad (Jean Tilho). *Colonel Tilho discovered these drawings on a rock formation in an oasis near Borkou, a northern Chad region centered around the town of Faya. The area is a sandy desert, part of the southwestern Sahara.*

Tilho and his military command broke Sanusi control over Borkou in 1913–1914. The Sanusi, a seminomadic Muslim sultinate, was historically important as a crossing place in the trans-Saharan trade between West Africa and Libya. Also, West African pilgrimages to Mecca passed through the sultinate. Although the French occupied Faya, they considered the region ungovernable. They withdrew their military administration in 1965. Tilho's finding of these rock drawings, in which hippopotami, horses, dogs, and ostriches are represented, further convinced him that a flourishing civilization, now buried beneath the desert sands, had existed along an ancient river that linked Lake Chad to the Nile.

destination of free slaves from the Americas at the end of the eighteenth century.

Nationalist-minded political activists demanded and won, piecemeal, self-rule during the late 1940s and 1950s. After it became an independent nation within the British Commonwealth in 1961 (it did not become an official republic until 1971), Sierra Leone enjoyed prosperity for a time. Much of the reason: its uniquely valuable mineral resources. Sierra Leone is a land literally sparkling with diamonds. Gems found along its riverbeds make it one of the world's leading diamond-producing countries.

Following an unhappy pattern in Third World countries, military officers took over the Sierra Leone government in 1967. Astonishingly, soldiers of lower rank soon mutinied. They threw coup leaders in jail and gave power back to an elected government headed by Siaka Stevens.

Sadly, the new government was a harsh one, quelling political opposition sometimes with violence. The country's government—as well as its diamond industry—was ravaged by corruption. Depletion of other natural resources led to an economic downturn. Open dissension escalated among the citizens, resulting in even tighter government restrictions. When Stevens retired in 1985, he turned control over to army chief Joseph Saidu Momoh.

In a 1992 coup, Momoh was ousted in the first of several military takeovers that rocked the Sierra Leone government during the 1990s. A 1997 power crisis prompted Nigeria and other West African republics to send in armed forces and restore embattled Ahmad Tejan Kabbah to the presidency. Guerilla opposition followed, but Kabbah remained head of state as of 2001.

Although many natives work the riverbeds and swamps in search of diamonds during the dry season, most are subsistence farmers. Poverty is especially rampant outside the country's capital and large towns. English is the official language, but many people speak in local tongues, and most practice native religions.

TOGO

A strange, thin finger of land protruding inland from the lower West African coast, Togo is a tropical nation unique among its West African neighbors. Though populated by citizens of different tribal origins, Togo is regarded not so much as a melting pot of traditional peoples, like some of the other former colonies, but rather as the scene of a major division of what once was a large kingdom. When the European powers drew their colonial boundary lines, the Ewe people were split. About half of them now live in Togo, and half in Ghana, the neighboring country to the west.

The Ewe language remains prominent in Togo, though French is the official language. The republic has patterned its educational system after that in France. Almost three fourths of the people have kept their ancient religions.

Faya, c. 1912–1917 (Jean Tilho).   *The oasis of Faya was chosen in 1913 as the military and adminis-trative center of what was then the region of French Borkou because it could be joined by wireless radio to the nearest French post in Chad, 350 miles away. The huts in this photograph were constructed from unbaked bricks. It took Tilho and his soldiers several months to build a sufficient number of them and to finish the necessary defensive arrangements. Those arrangements consisted of three rows of rope, barbed by adding long thorns from date trees (center of photograph).*

   At the edge of this encampment were rows of date palms (rear of photograph), broken at intervals by heaps of moving sand dunes. The green meadow on either side of the palm groves was covered with a sharp, hard grass. Jackals and gazelles were the only wild animals in the area.

Togo's vegetation includes savanna grasslands, tropical forests, and on the coast, mangrove swamps. Lomé, on the Gulf of Guinea, is Togo's seaport/capital. Most of the country's people farm for their livelihoods; Togo exports comparatively few crops. Phosphate and limestone mining generate most of the republic's income.

   Although it is hemmed tightly by neighboring countries, Togo has been something of a loner among West African nations. Its military regime after independence made little effort to cooperate with other governments, and the predominant lifestyle is fairly primitive. Its president, Gnassingbé Eyadéma, has been in office since 1967. Opponents cry foul play in elections, and Togo was the scene of political violence and deaths during the 1990s. Thousands of Togo residents have fled to neighboring Benin and Ghana.

WESTERN SAHARA

If you have trouble finding information about Western Sahara or, as it formerly was known, Spanish Sahara, you might look under "Morocco." Morocco lays claim to this desert coastal neighbor—but the issue has been under dispute for years. Spanish explorers and traders visited the Sahara coast centuries ago. In the late 1860s Spain more or less formally possessed this, its lone holding in colonial Africa. In 1976, with practically all the other European influences already withdrawn from Africa, Spain relinquished its so-called Province of Spanish Sahara into the control of neighboring countries. Morocco got the northern area, Mauritania the south.

A lot of people living in what then became known as Western Sahara, however, opposed this division. Calling themselves the Polisario Front and aided by Algeria to the east, they wanted to have their own country. The territory was embroiled in civil war. In 1979 Mauritania withdrew. Moroccan forces exerted control in the cities, but Polisario rebels roamed freely in the rocky, sparsely vegetated desert expanse.

The United Nations fashioned a cease-fire in 1991, hoping to oversee a popular vote on the question of independence versus Moroccan rule. The referendum, at this writing, has yet to be arranged. U.N. forces continue to patrol the country.

With its capital at the port of Laayoune, Western Sahara has a population of about 300,000. Most citizens, descendants of ancient Arab and Berber peoples, are nomads who herd goats, sheep, camels, and other livestock. Fishers in coastal villages roam the ocean waters. Phosphates are the country's main natural resource.

Dunes, Northern Chad, c. 1912–1917 (Jean Tilho). *Colonel Tilho observed how moving, wind-driven, burning sand dunes (front of photograph) engulfed rock outcroppings. He believed that evidence of an ancient civilization was buried under such dunes. The size and depth of wells, natural cisterns, and archaeological evidence of fish fossils and dried-up river beds further added to Tilho's eventual conclusion that an ancient river had connected Lake Chad with the Nile.*

West African Republics Grope for a Place in the World

At present, no light is visible at the end of the region's long, dark tunnel leading from strife to prosperity. By and large, West Africa's people simply are learning to adjust to a hard life—not altogether unlike their ancient ancestors did. But their challenges and hardships are more complex than ever. Their bush and jungle today encompass not just the lands their forebears knew so well, but an outside world fueled by industry, technology, and superpower politics and economies. That outside world is basically a hostile one that has never fully embraced West Africa as part of itself.

Nakazas, Chad, c. 1912–1917 (Jean Tilho).   *Tilho photographed these nomadic Nakazas dancing at an oasis in Borkou. The entire population of this desert region was under 10,000. Tilho observed that camel caravans from southern Chad loaded up with dates and salt from nearby pits and gave the Nakazas cereals, butter, cattle, and smoke-dried meat in return.*

8

WEST
AFRICA
TODAY

West Africa is a product of its past—both recent and distant. In the cities, you see the influences of industrialization: modern buildings, business offices, stores, restaurants, public parks, and traffic jams. As in Europe and America, those who are well off live in nice residences. Those who are poor live in slums. "Shanty towns" stand on the outskirts of cities, populated by country families who have moved in seeking (but rarely finding) better living conditions.

Close outside the urban areas, the bush country and its tribes exist much as in centuries past. Most West Africans live off the land. They make simple shelters of mud walls and straw roofs, or of modern materials like concrete or rusty iron sheets, if available. They make their own basic tools and clothes, and farm small plots of staple crops for their families or tribes.

In Senegal, a typical Wolof village may have a hundred people—all farmers living in simple huts. The village typically has a small mosque, a shaded commons, a nearby stream or well (perhaps a narrow canal dug along the perimeter of houses for the public water supply), and on the outskirts, crop storage buildings made of straw.

Around the "bulge" in the Republic of Benin, you find small villages with houses made of "waddle," sticks woven together with mud plaster. The natives carve stools, masks, tools, and other items from wood. In Côte d'Ivoire and Sierra Leone, towns come alive on market day, when tribal women peddle yams, cassava roots, nuts, and vegetables. In coastal lagoons, fishers sell their daily catch. Far to the north in Mali and other arid areas, farming people live in domed, straw-thatched houses. Among the nomads, women sew tents of woven wool.

Each West African country consists of numerous religious and ethnic peoples speaking varied languages. Most people in West Africa belong to one of three major language groups. Semito-Hamitic languages are spoken mainly among the Arabs and Berbers in the north. Niger-Congo languages are common in the south, except in portions of the Niger basin and the Lake Chad area. There, we hear Nilo-Saharan languages, similar to those of northeastern Africa.

When petroleum was discovered in the Niger delta, it was exciting news for the economy of Nigeria—but a disaster for the fishers who lived there, as pollution decimated underwater wildlife.

Let's make a brief overview of modern West Africa.

RESOURCES, INDUSTRY, AND AGRICULTURE

Gone from West Africa are most of the incentives that brought early European explorers to the region. To their credit, the whites eventually outlawed slavery. But among the permanent damage done by whites, in this case by way of their native middlemen, were the decimation of the elephant population and the plundering of some natural resources. Phosphates and other minerals continue to be mined in significant quantities, and a wide array of agricultural products, from cocoa to peanuts to cotton, is exported.

Health

Hospitals and health clinics have increased across modern West Africa, but overall, health care is inadequate. Diseases that were practically eradicated long ago in industrial countries still plague certain parts of West Africa. Examples are leprosy, malaria, and worms causing stomach disorders. Throughout West Africa, the infant mortality rate is high—around 12 percent.

The best health care, as you would expect, is obtained in the cities. The death rate in rural areas is many times higher than in urban centers.

Transportation

Most of West Africa's road-and-rail system originated in the colonial era. Lines of transportation were built from seaports like Dakar, Freetown, Abidjan, and Lagos to trade centers (typically river ports) in the interior. The railways are generally outdated, but the republics have no funds to make substantial improvements. Relatively few roads are paved, and many are impassable in rainy seasons.

Nigeria is fairly advanced among the West African countries in transportation progress. There, most thoroughfares connecting major towns and cities are paved, though local roads typically are dirt. Nigeria even boasts a freeway between Lagos and Ibadan, its two largest cities. By contrast, Mauritania to the west, though larger than Nigeria, has only about a thousand miles of paved roads connecting its mostly desert-surrounded towns.

Along the lower coast of the "bulge," a picturesque highway stretches between Ghana and Benin.

Air transport in West Africa is limited mostly to regional flights. But large cities like Dakar, Lagos, and Lomé have international airports.

Education

One of the first objectives of practically every new African republic was educational improvement. Free and mandatory elementary school attendance became common across the continent. New colleges were built. Unhappily, success was limited in most scenarios. Sierra Leone, for one, does not require public school attendance. Even in countries where elementary education is mandated, much of the school-age population does not attend.

Critics suggest that some independent African nations never have cast off certain fundamental vestiges of colonial influence. For example, courses in some of the former French colonial schools still are taught in French; students in certain formerly British-run schools still are taught in English. "Africanization" of education in independent Africa, in sum, has lagged. The emphasis still seems to be on providing Western-style education, geared toward western interests and goals.

Regionwide, schools are not on a par with those of most industrial nations. Some countries—Senegal, for one—have recently taken significant steps to expand education at all levels and to press for higher attendance in rural villages. The University of Dakar in Senegal has been a leader in "Africanizing" its operation, focusing on African-oriented courses and evolving a faculty consisting mostly of Africans. It draws many students from neighboring countries.

As with health care and other conveniences in living conditions, education is more readily available to West Africans living in or near cities than country villages. Literacy rates vary widely, from less than 20 percent of the population in Mali and Burkina Faso to about 60 percent in Ghana. But overall, West Africans can take heart in the fact that literacy rates have multiplied since independence, and many new schools of higher learning have been built.

ECONOMIC CONDITIONS

In the economy lies the taproot of West Africa's problems. (Bear in mind that numerous factors inside and outside Africa affect the continent's economic health.) Before the Europeans came, tribes hunted, foraged, and grew what food and other products they needed locally. By and large, their livelihoods were quite meager by western standards. But the people were content. Peace and happiness were broken mainly by raids between traditional tribal enemies and natural disasters (droughts, floods, plagues).

Itinerant Merchants, Chad, c. 1912–1917 (Jean Tilho). *Two itinerant merchants, wearing white, are photographed with two of Tilho's soldiers in Borkou, the desert region of northern Chad. The more fertile oases in this sparsely populated area grew dates and vegetables. Salt, though, was the commodity that merchants sought—with caravans of 200 camels or so being loaded up at local pits. The lucrative slave trade through Borkou ceased under French control.*

The Europeans claimed they were coming to help the Africans solve those kinds of problems. In the end, they made admirable progress in eliminating or reducing the impact of deadly diseases in many regions. But they left the African nations in a complex economic morass that defied the efforts of the new governments to solve.

Cooperation between the republics is one key to solving the problems. The Niger River Commission was formed in 1963. Its objective is to study and promote river travel and commerce, especially along the middle stretches of the Niger. Similarly, Mali, Mauritania, and Senegal have cooperated in building hydroelectric stations on the River Senegal. Their union is called the Organization for the Development of the Senegal River. In the southwest, Liberia, Sierra Leone, and Guinea have formed the Mano River Union to promote mutual economic interests.

West Africans also wisely have banded together to protect their natural resources. Benin, Niger, and Burkina Faso jointly protect the "W" National Park, a wildlife reserve of almost 3 million acres—one of the largest reserves on the continent. To the west, the Mount Nimba Reserve was established by Côte d'Ivoire, Guinea, and Liberia to protect wildlife in a blend of rainforest and savanna terrain.

RELIGIONS

Typically, peoples in the Saharan and sub-Saharan areas are Muslims, influenced by the influx of Arabs who fanned across northern Africa many centuries ago. In coastal cities of the sub-Saharan "bulge," Christianity is strong—the result of Protestant mission efforts dating to the 1700s and Catholic missions that began in the early years of European exploration.

In the heart of the tropics, tribes generally follow ancient religious beliefs and superstitions. For example, the Mende people of Sierra Leone look for small, carved figures called *nomoli,* which archaeologists believe date from the fifteenth century, buried in the ground. *Nomoli* are thought to bring farmers abundant crops.

It's not uncommon across West Africa to find a melding of religious thought. Old tribal ceremonies and beliefs might be combined with more recent teachings of Christianity or Islam.

CULTURE AND ENTERTAINMENT

West Africa's cultural diversity has been shaped mainly by the distinctions between "city life" and "country life." American and European influences have greatly affected the literature, music, and art of city dwellers. Traditional ceremonies and music (largely based on ancient customs and superstitions) and oral story-telling are alive and largely unchanged in the bush.

Americans who spend time among West African peoples are impressed by their frequent music making. Skin drums, tin cans, and other percussion instruments; primitive but artistically carved wood flutes; crude stringed instruments with gourd and shell backs . . . these are played solo or in small ensembles,

Koussadas, c. 1912–1917 (Jean Tilho). *Almost 125 miles north of Faya, after a seven-day trek across the Chad desert, Tilho reached Mount Koussi, the highest summit in the Sahara. It is an extinct volcano with a crater approximately twelve miles wide. He spent sixteen days exploring the mountain, making extensive mathematical calculations. One of Tilho's explorer-heroes, the German Gustav Nachtigal, had been the first European to scale Mount Koussi (1870). Tilho used Nachtigal's account as a reference work.*

Colonel Tilho encountered about 200–300 Koussadas (named by Nachtigal) living miserably in caves along the mountain slopes. Their staple food was a wild herb that grew among the rocks. It yielded a coarse flour that resembled coal dust. At times these people killed a kind of wild mountain sheep for food.

sometimes accompanying chants and songs. The musicians typically are professionals who often practice all day long. They perform at ritual events (weddings, birth celebrations). They accompany laborers with work songs. And as you might expect, their music is vital to religious ceremonies. Their ancestral gods, the people believe, delight in music and dance. The more spirited, the better.

Nigeria, drawing influences from native black, Arabic, and western sources, is especially rich in its cultural heritage.

Stephen Jay, whose field recordings of West African music were published in America in the 1970s, described a night-time street dance in a Nigerian Songhai village:

> Six *gulu* drummers pound out the powerful rhythms that incite villagers to dramatic, near-hysterical solo dancing. A small circle formed by the spectators is presided over by the leader of the drummers, who collects money from each dancer for the music and, during the dancing itself, stomps around the circle screaming and beating the ground with a stick, as though overwhelmed with rage.

Jay further observed that the West African bush people "depend on music to nourish nearly every phase of their lives."

Many city residents have radio, televisions, and telephones. Electronic means of communication and entertainment are rare in rural areas. Mauritania, a country of about 2.5 million people, is estimated to have no more than 6,000 telephones. Niger has one phone for every 650–700 citizens.

Some media are run by private companies, some by the government. In The Gambia, the country's single newspaper is a government organ, as is Radio Gambia. The governments of Mali and other republics also keep close control over news media.

Life Goes On

Ruined national economies and international trade deficits, illiteracy and poverty, sometimes-violent struggles between tribes and religions . . . this is the picture of West Africa we see in the news today. But for the people there, life goes on. While governments rise and fall above them and calamities, both natural and human-caused, storm around them, many people in West Africa still live much like their ancient ancestors.

Historian Basil Davidson observed,

> Most of the continent's populations, cut off from the outside world by seas of sand and water, had worked out pre-industrial ways of living that were adequate to survival and

Tilho Guide, c. 1912–1917 (Jean Tilho). *During 1912–1917, Colonel Jean Tilho crossed northern Chad, the western border of the Libyan desert, and the Kordofan of the Sudan to the Nile River at Khartoum—always making planetary observations and mapping key landmarks in his attempt to prove that an ancient river connected Lake Chad with the Nile.*

After five years in Central Africa, Tilho announced to an October 1920 meeting of the Royal Geographical Society that "the great geographical problem of ancient fluvial communication between the basins of the Chad and the Nile is definitely solved . . . proved by the agreement of geological, topographical, ichthyological, malacological, and other observations made in these regions."

Tilho repeatedly paid tribute to his native guides who persevered with him through horrendous desert areas, areas where both men and their camels became exhausted by the crushing heat and where supplies of food and water were extremely limited.

even to a fair degree of comfort. Real information is scant, but the available evidence suggests that most peoples south of the Sahara had a standard of living far above the minimum subsistence level, and enjoyed a reasonably secure life.

Colonization and industrialization turned that world upside-down . . . but did not destroy it completely. The challenge for West Africa's leaders now is to compete, cooperate, and survive in the digital space age while clinging to the strengths the great continent gave their ancestors.

CHRONOLGY

A.D. 1000	Arab merchants arrive in western Africa.
1470	Portuguese traders establish outposts along the Gulf of Guinea. Other Europeans follow them to the region.
Circa 1700	Slaves become one of West Africa's major exports.
Late 1700s	Protestant societies in Europe begin to send missionaries to West Africa. Catholic leaders expand their own African mission work, begun centuries earlier in the region.
1787	England establishes a colony of former slaves at Sierra Leone.
1807	Great Britain outlaws slavery; soon, it posts warships off the West African coast to block slave traffic from the continent.
1822–24	Freed slaves from America establish the country of Liberia.
1884	Spain establishes control over Western (Spanish) Sahara.
1884–85	European leaders discuss their interests in specific African territories at the West African Conference, held in Berlin. In the eyes of some historians, the great European powers in effect "partitioned" Africa.
1886	The British government charters the Royal Niger Company for trading.
Circa 1890–1914	France and England establish their colonial administrations in West Africa, sometimes subduing native resistance by force.
By 1895	France has begun "administering" vast territories in what becomes known as French West Africa.
1890s	The Aborigines' Rights Protection Society, one of the forerunners of West African independence movements, is formed.
1900	The first Pan-African Conference is held in London.
1914	With the advent of World War I, thousands of black West Africans are pressed into service to fight in Europe.
1930s	West African activists begin organizing political parties and push for independence.
1939	World War II prompts European armies to use black Africans once more to fight in Europe.
1957	The Gold Coast colony of Great Britain becomes a sovereign country, though it remains within the British Commonwealth. Three years later, it becomes the independent Republic of Ghana. Other former British colonies follow in the mass transition to an independent Africa.

1958	France grants its African colonies self-governing status as members of the French Community. By 1960, the former French colonies are establishing full independence.
1974-75	Portugal grants independence to Guinea-Bissau and Cape Verde.
1976	Spain withdraws from Spanish Sahara, leaving a "no man's land" whose sovereignty remains contested by warring forces within and outside the former colony.
Circa 1960–present	West African nations grapple with ethnic clashes, natural catastrophes, political power struggles, inadequate natural resources, adverse world markets, and other problems in establishing their places as independent nations of the world community.

GLOSSARY

annexation—bringing new territory (usually adjoining land) into an existing government or corporate entity

arable—suitable for farming

archaeologist—one who studies and preserves past human remains

aristocratic—having to do with a country's upper or ruling class

bearer—a native employed by an expedition to carry supplies (same as **porter**)

bush—remote, little-populated terrain, often thick with undergrowth

caravan—a convoy of travelers and transport animals or vehicles; camel caravans are still used in parts of Africa

cash crop—a crop grown for quick sale locally, rather than for long-term storage or export

coalition—a usually short-term union of political factions

coup—a political take-over, which may be violent or peaceful

entrepreneur—a person or company who plans and carries out a potentially profitable business venture, often at a financial risk

equator—the imaginary east-west circle around the earth at approximately its thickest central part, half-way between the poles

ethnic—having to do with the culture, religion, language, race, etc., of a distinct group of people

federation—a union or league of countries

fez—a flat-topped, felt hat worn by men in certain Mediterranean and African desert countries

hinterland—the region inland from a coast, often suggesting a remote, hard-to-reach area

hydroelectric power—electrical power generated by fast-flowing water

industrialized nations—countries—notably western nations—whose economies are based on highly developed industries

mangrove swamp—a tropical swamp notable for its mangrove shrubs whose stilted roots rise above the surface of the water

modus operandi—method of operations

mosque—place of worship for Muslims

nomad—a wanderer; a member of a tribe or group who move from one area to another with seasonal changes, herding or hunting

oasis—an "island of life" in a desert, with water and plants

porter—see **bearer**

rainforest—dense tropical forest with rich plant and animal life, usually situated near the equator, made lush and humid by high amounts annual rainfall

GLOSSARY

repatriate—to return an enslaved or displaced citizen to his/her homeland

republic—a country ruled not by a king or queen, but by an elected government (military factions and dictators have seized power in many African republics)

ritual—a detailed, traditional procedure for a religious, familial, or cultural ceremony

sanctions—in cases such as that of Uganda under Idi Amin, international measures (often economic) to pressure a country to end broad-scale legal violations or inhumane practices

savanna—a region of grasslands, with sparse shrubs and trees

steppe—a semidry, grassy plain

sub-Sahara—the geographical buffer region of Africa lying between the Sahara Desert in the north and the continent's central tropics

subsistence farming—growing just enough crops to provide for the needs of a family or tribe

treaty—a formal trading and/or peace agreement between nations or, as in Africa during colonization, between European powers or trading companies and important native chiefs

tropics—the hot, humid zone near the equator

WORLD WITHOUT END

DEIRDRE SHIELDS

ONE SUMMER'S DAY in 1830, a group of Englishmen met in London and decided to start a learned society to promote "that most important and entertaining branch of knowledge—Geography," and the Royal Geographical Society (RGS) was born.

The society was formed by the Raleigh Travellers' Club, an exclusive dining club, whose members met over exotic meals to swap tales of their travels. Members included Lord Broughton, who had travelled with the poet Byron, and John Barrow, who had worked in the iron foundries of Liverpool before becoming a force in the British Admiralty.

From the start, the Royal Geographical Society led the world in exploration, acting as patron and inspiration for the great expeditions to Africa, the Poles, and the Northwest Passage, that elusive sea connection between the Atlantic and Pacific. In the scramble to map the world, the society embodied the spirit of the age: that English exploration was a form of benign conquest.

The society's gold medal awards for feats of exploration read like a Who's Who of famous explorers, among them David Livingstone, for his 1855 explorations in Africa; the American explorer Robert Peary, for his 1898 discovery of the "northern termination of the Greenland ice"; Captain Robert Scott, the first Englishman to reach the South Pole, in 1912; and on and on.

Today the society's headquarters, housed in a red-brick Victorian lodge in South Kensington, still has the effect of a gentleman's club, with courteous staff, polished wood floors, and fine paintings.

West Africa

The building archives the world's most important collection of private exploration papers, maps, documents, and artefacts. Among the RGS's treasures are the hats Livingstone and Henry Morton Stanley wore at their famous meeting ("Dr. Livingstone, I presume?") at Ujiji in 1871, and the chair the dying Livingstone was carried on during his final days in Zambia. The collection also includes models of expedition ships, paintings, dug-out canoes, polar equipment, and Charles Darwin's pocket sextant.

The library's 500,000 images cover the great moments of exploration. Here is Edmund Hillary's shot of Sherpa Tenzing standing on Everest. Here is Captain Lawrence Oates, who deliberately walked out of his tent in a blizzard to his death because his illness threatened to delay Captain Scott's party. Here, too is the American Museum of Natural History's 1920 expedition across the Gobi Desert in dusty convoy (the first to drive motorised vehicles across a desert).

The day I visited, curator Francis Herbert was trying to find maps for five different groups of adventurers at the same time from the largest private map collection in the world. Among the 900,000 items are maps dating to 1482 and ones showing the geology of the moon and thickness of ice in Antarctica, star atlases, and "secret" topographic maps from the former Soviet Union.

The mountaineer John Hunt pitched a type of base camp in a room at the RGS when he organised the 1953 Everest expedition that put Hillary and Tenzing on top of the world. "The society was my base, and source of my encouragement," said the late Lord Hunt, who noted that the nature of that work is different today from what it was when he was the society's president from 1976 to 1980. "When I was involved, there was still a lot of genuine territorial exploration to be done. Now, virtually every important corner—of the land surface, at any rate—has been discovered, and exploration has become more a matter of detail, filling in the big picture."

The RGS has shifted from filling in blanks on maps to providing a lead for the new kind of exploration, under the banner of geography: "I see exploration not so much as a question of 'what' and 'where' anymore, but 'why' and 'how': How does the earth work, the environment function, and how do we manage our resources sustainably?" says the society's director, Dr. Rita Gardner. "Our role today is to answer such questions at the senior level of scientific research," Gardner continues, "through our big, multidisciplinary expeditions, through the smaller expeditions we support and encourage, and by advancing the subject of geography, advising governments, and encouraging wider public understanding. Geography is the subject of the 21st century because it embraces everything—peoples, cultures, landscapes, environments—and pulls them all together."

The society occupies a unique position in world-class exploration. To be invited to speak at the RGS is still regarded as an accolade, the ultimate seal of approval of Swan, who in 1989 became the first person to walk to both the North and South Poles, and who says, "The hairs still stand on the back of my neck when I think about the first time I spoke at the RGS. It was the greatest honour."

The RGS set Swan on the path of his career as an explorer, assisting him with a 1979 expedition retracing Scott's journey to the South Pole. "I was a Mr. Nobody, trying to raise seven million dollars, and getting nowhere," says Swan. "The RGS didn't tell me I was mad—they gave me access to Scott's private papers. From those, I found fifty sponsors who had supported Scott, and persuaded them to fund me. On the basis of a photograph I found of one of his chaps sitting on a box of 'Shell Spirit,' I got Shell to sponsor the fuel for my ship."

The name "Royal Geographical Society" continues to open doors. Although the society's actual membership—some 12,600 "fellows," as they are called—is small, the organisation offers an incomparable network of people, experience, and expertise. This is seen in the work of the Expeditionary Advisory Centre. The EAC was established in 1980 to provide a focus for would-be explorers. If you want to know how to raise sponsorship, handle snakes safely, or find a mechanic for your trip across the Sahara, the EAC can help. Based in Lord Hunt's old Everest office, the EAC funds some 50 small expeditions a year and offers practical training and advice to hundreds more. Its safety tips range from the pragmatic—"In subzero temperatures, metal spectacle frames can cause frostbite (as can earrings and nose-rings)"—to the unnerving—"Remember: A decapitated snake head can still bite."

The EAC is unique, since it is the only centre in the world that helps small-team, low-budget expeditions, thus keeping the amateur—in the best sense of the word—tradition of exploration alive.

"The U.K. still sends out more small expeditions per capita than any other country," says Dr. John Hemming, director of the RGS from 1975 to 1996. During his tenure, Hemming witnessed the growth in exploration-travel. "In the 1960s we'd be dealing with 30 to 40 expeditions a year. By 1997 it was 120, but the quality hadn't gone down—it had gone up. It's a boom time for exploration, and the RGS is right at the heart of it."

While the EAC helps adventure-travellers, it concentrates its funding on scientific field research projects, mostly at the university level. Current projects range from studying the effect of the pet trade on Madagscar's chameleons, to mapping uncharted terrain in the south Ecuadorian cloud forest. Jen Hurst is a typical "graduate" of the EAC. With two fellow Oxford students, she received EAC technical training, support, and a $2,000 grant to do biological surveys in the Kyabobo Range, a new national park in Ghana.

"The RGS's criteria for funding are very strict," says Hurst. "They put you through a real grilling, once you've made your application. They're very tough on safety, and very keen on working alongside people from the host country. The first thing they wanted to be sure of was whether we would involve local students. They're the leaders of good practice in the research field."

When Hurst and her colleagues returned from Ghana in 1994, they presented a case study of their work at an EAC seminar. Their talk prompted a $15,000 award from the BP oil company for them to set up a registered charity, the Kyabobo Conservation Project, to ensure that work in the park continues, and that followup ideas for community-based conservation, social, and education projects are developed. "It's been a great experience, and crucial to the careers we hope to make in environmental work," says Hurst. "And it all started through the RGS."

The RGS is rich in prestige but it is not particularly wealthy in financial terms. Compared to the National Geographic Society in the U.S., the RGS is a pauper. However, bolstered by sponsorship from such companies as British Airways and Discovery Channel Europe, the RGS remains one of Britain's largest organisers of geographical field research overseas.

The ten major projects the society has undertaken over the last 20 or so years have spanned the world, from Pakistan and Oman to Brunei and Australia. The scope is large—hundreds of people are currently working in the field and the emphasis is multidisciplinary, with the aim to break down traditional barriers, not only among the different strands of science but also among nations. This is exploration as The Big Picture, preparing blueprints for governments around the globe to work on. For example, the 1977 Mulu (Sarawak) expedition to Borneo was credited with kick-starting the international concern for tropical rain forests.

The society's three current projects include water and soil erosion studies in Nepal, sustainable land use in Jordan, and a study of the Mascarene Plateau in the western Indian Ocean, to develop ideas on how best to conserve ocean resources in the future.

Projects adhere to a strict code of procedure. "The society works only at the invitation of host governments and in close co-operation with local people," explains Winser. "The findings are published in the host countries first, so they can get the benefit. Ours are long-term projects, looking at processes and trends, adding to the sum of existing knowledge, which is what exploration is about."

Exploration has never been more fashionable in England. More people are travelling adventurously on their own account, and the RGS's increasingly younger membership (the average age has dropped in the last 20 years from over 45 to the early 30s) is exploration-literate and able to make the fine distinctions between adventure / extreme / expedition / scientific travel.

Rebecca Stephens, who in 1993 became the first British woman to summit Everest, says she "pops along on Monday evenings to listen to the lectures." These occasions are sociable, informal affairs, where people find themselves talking to such luminaries as explorer Sir Wilfred Thesiger, who attended Haile Selassie's coronation in Ethiopia in 1930, or David Puttnam, who produced the film *Chariots of Fire* and is a vice president of the RGS. Shortly before his death, Lord Hunt was spotted in deep conversation with the singer George Michael.

Summing up the society's enduring appeal, Shane Winser says, "The Royal Geographical Society is synonymous with exploration, which is seen as something brave and exciting. In a sometimes dull, depressing world, the Royal Geographical Society offers a spirit of adventure people are always attracted to."

FURTHER READING

Chételat, Eleanor de. "My Domestic Life in French Guinea." *National Geographic,* June 1935, p. 695.

Davidson, Basil. *A History of West Africa to the Nineteenth Century.* Garden City, NY: Anchor Books. 1966.

Davidson, Basil, *et al. African Kingdoms* ("Great Ages of Man" series). New York: Time-Life Books. 1966.

Fichter, George S. *The Bulge of Africa.* New York: Franklin Watts. 1981.

French, George K. "The Gold Coast, Ashanti, and Kumassi." *National Geographic,* January 1897, p. 1.

Harmon, Daniel E. *Nigeria, 1880 to the Present: The Struggle, the Tragedy, the Promise* ("Exploration of Africa: The Emerging Nations" series) Philadelphia: Chelsea House Publishers. 2000.

Jay, Stephen. "Africa Drum, Chant & Instrumental Music" (field recordings and notes from Niger, Mali, Upper Volta). New York: Nonesuch Records. 1976.

Koslow, Philip. *Centuries of Greatness—The West African Kingdoms: 750–1900* ("Milestones in Black American History" series). New York/Philadelphia: Chelsea House Publishers. 1995.

Nelson, Harold D., ed. *Liberia: A Country Study.* Washington: Department of the Army. 1984.

Outhwaite, Leonard. *Unrolling the Map: The Story of Exploration.* New York: John Day/Reynal & Hitchcock. 1935.

Packenham, Thomas. *The Scramble for Africa: 1876–1912.* New York: Random House. 1991.

Priest, Cecil D. "Timbuktu, in the Sands of the Sahara." *National Geographic,* January 1924, p. 73.

Rabot, Dr. Charles. "Recent French Explorations in Africa." *National Geographic,* April 1902, p. 119.

Shillington, Kevin. *Independence in Africa* ("Causes and Consequences" series). Austin, TX: Steck-Vaugh Company. 1998.

Talbot, P.A. "Notes on the Ekoi." *National Geographic,* January 1912, p. 33.

Theobald, Robert, ed. *The New Nations of West Africa.* New York: The H.W. Wilson Company. 1960.

Webster, J.B., and A.A. Boahen. *History of West Africa: The Revolutionary Years—1815 to Independence.* New York: Praeger Publishers. 1970.

INDEX

INDEX

INDEX

INDEX

INDEX

INDEX

INDEX

INDEX

INDEX

ABOUT THE AUTHORS

Dr. Richard E. Leakey is a distinguished paleo-anthropologist and conservationist. He is chairman of the Wildlife Clubs of Kenya Association and the Foundation for the Research into the Origins of Man. He presented the BBC-TV series *The Making of Mankind* (1981) and wrote the accompanying book. His other publications include *People of the Lake* (1979) and *One Life* (1984). Richard Leakey, along with his famous parents, Louis and Mary, was named by *Time* magazine as one of the greatest minds of the twentieth century.

Daniel E. Harmon is an editor and writer living in Spartanburg, South Carolina. The author of several books on history, he has contributed historical and cultural articles to *The New York Times, Music Journal, Nautilus,* and many other periodicals. He is the associate editor of *Sandlapper: The Magazine of South Carolina* and editor of *The Lawyer's PC* newsletter.

Deirdre Shields is the author of many articles dealing with contemporary life in Great Britain. Her essays have appeared in *The Times*, *The Daily Telegraph*, *Harpers & Queen*, and *The Field.*